UNDERSTANDI
THE PRE

Encountering
the God who Heals

John Ryeland

21 20 19 18 17   7 6 5 4 3 2 1

First published in 2017 by Malcolm Down Publishing Ltd
www.malcolmdown.co.uk

British Library Cataloguing in Publication Data

A catalogue record for this book is available from the British Library.

ISBN 978-1-910786-73-4

Cover design by Esther Kotecha
Additional photography by Sarah Grace
Printed in the UK

CONTENTS

Foreword by Charles Whitehead   v

Introduction   ix

Part 1: Discovering Who We Are

  1. Who Do You Think You Are?   3

  2. God's Heart Revealed   5

  3. Speaking His Blessing Over Us   11

  4. Four Truths from Ephesians 1   12

  5. Making the Truth Real to Us   22

  6. Being a Name-bearer   24

  7. Practising Being a Name-bearer   32

Part 2: Meeting Jesus in Encounter Prayer

  8. It's All About the Encounter   37

  9. Trying it for Ourselves   65

Part 3: Letting Jesus Heal Through Us

  10. Recalling Who We Are   71

  11. Is Healing a Gift?   75

  12. What Makes a Good Prayer Minister?   77

  13. Beginning by Listening   84

  14. The Three Aspects of Healing Prayer   88

  15. No Guarantees   121

  16. Can We Get in the Way?   126

  17. Listening to What God Says for Others   128

  18. Working Together as a Team   133

  19. Intercession   135

  20. Final Thoughts   138

Appendix 1: Summary of Meditations   143

Appendix 2: Encountering Jesus on Your Own   149

Appendix 3: Encountering Jesus with a Group   153

Appendix 4: Guidelines for Ministry   161

FOREWORD

John Ryeland has been actively involved in the healing ministry for many years, a number of them as Director of the London-based Christian Healing Mission. To understand the context in which he is exercising this important ministry and in which *Encountering the God Who Heals* has been written, I believe it will be helpful to remind ourselves of the way the Holy Spirit has been at work in the life of the church in recent years.

Church historians are already speaking of the twentieth century as *The Century of the Holy Spirit.* The Holy Spirit has always been at work in the church since the Day of Pentecost, but in the early twentieth century there were clear signs of new outpourings of his love and power in Topeka, Kansas, in the Welsh Revival, and most powerfully in the events at a small, run-down mission church in Azusa Street, Los Angeles, which came to be looked upon as the birthplace of Pentecostalism. As new Pentecostal churches sprang up all over the world, the Spirit also began to stir up new life in the main-line Protestant denominations in the 1960s, in the Roman Catholic Church from 1967, and brought to birth hundreds of new Independent Charismatic Churches in the 1970s and 80s. Signs and wonders once again became a normal part of the Christian life and healings, miracles, prophecies, tongues, expectant faith and words of knowledge all became regular features of church services and Christian gatherings, as the Holy Spirit distributed his charisms freely among the faithful in every walk of life.

Against this background, a real need arose for good teachers who could explain, encourage and pastor the exercise of all these charismatic gifts of the Spirit, but particularly his gifts of healings which, quite understandably, often attracted the greatest interest. We all owe a debt of gratitude to men like Francis McNutt, the late John Wimber, and more recently Bill Johnson, who have modelled and encouraged the ministry of healing. In a similar way, John Ryeland is playing a very important part by promoting a correct understanding and practice of the healing ministry today. He does this by giving sound teaching and offering accessible models to all Christians who are engaged in praying for healing in local parishes and fellowships.

In *Encountering the God Who Heals* John shows a remarkable understanding of just what lies at the heart of this ministry and how we should go about exercising it. His years of experience have given him a unique and immensely valuable perspective on ministering healing in the name of Jesus Christ in a variety of settings – always under the inspiration and in the power of the Holy Spirit. Many Christian books have been written on healing and all of them contain insights that are instructive for the reader, but I have never read one that is more solidly based, or more realistic and helpful than this one. The simple but essential truth that comes through page after page is that everything is rooted and grounded in the presence of Jesus Christ and in the depth of interaction that results.

> **. . . everything is rooted and grounded in the presence of Jesus Christ and in the depth of interaction that results**

The first part of the book, 'Discovering Who We Are', emphasises how absolutely essential it is to be certain about who we are in Christ and to really understand how much God loves us and how he looks upon us. Only when we have grasped this can everything else fall into its proper place. I'm delighted John started here because I know very well that there are still many Christians who do not yet fully understand what it means to be a child of God. Once we have this truth in our minds and hearts, we are ready for the second part of the book, 'Meeting Jesus in Encounter Prayer'. The encounter involves experiencing fellowship and relationship with Jesus which will lead us into an open and honest communication with him. These first two parts of the book are essential if we are to be fully open to the third part – 'Letting Jesus Heal'. Then, as we receive healing ourselves and are open to acting as channels for God's healing to others, we will benefit from the practical and sensible 'Guidelines for Ministry' outlined at the end of the book and offered to individuals, churches, prayer groups and healing teams to help them as they pray for healing. These guidelines, based on John's many years' experience of prayer ministry in a variety of settings, are enormously valuable.

Of all the books about healing I have read, *Encountering the God Who Heals* offers the best explanation of what is essential for a proper understanding of this ministry, which we are reminded can only begin when we really grasp who we are in Christ and seek his presence. John has done us all a great service by presenting these essential truths in a style that is attractive, easily readable, full of great wisdom, and based on years of practical, hands-on experience. *Encountering the God Who Heals* should be essential reading for every Christian who wants to know more about intimacy with God and the place of prayer in encountering the healing Jesus.

Charles Whitehead
Charles Whitehead was President of The International Catholic Charismatic Renewal Council for eleven years.

INTRODUCTION

In my role as Director of The Christian Healing Mission in Hammersmith, London, I have the enormous privilege of speaking to individuals and groups about the healing ministry. This always involves watching with amazement the wonderful things that God is doing, as well as often exploring with them why the healing they seek is not happening.

This book is an attempt to try to share something of what we have been discovering about the healing ministry – how it is so closely linked to finding the presence of God and seeing what can flow from him. Time and time again I am discovering the joy of leading people into the presence of Jesus through what we call 'encounter prayer', and standing amazed at the genuine depth of interaction between them and their Lord. My hope is that through **The focus is really us meeting with Jesus** this book more people can be touched by this ministry and find out how these encounters with Jesus can be 'a little bit life changing'.

Although this book is about what I have discovered since getting involved in the healing ministry, it is not just to do with healing in the sense of our symptoms being cured. The focus is really us meeting with Jesus. It is therefore also a book about prayer, an intimacy with God in which we can all share, and through that find the healing Jesus we long to meet.

The book is divided into three parts. The first part really looks at the sheer wonder of who we are. Without that realisation, we may find it hard to understand why God would ever touch someone like us. The second part explains something of what I have come to call 'Encounter Prayer', and encourages us all to enter into it for ourselves. The third part looks at how we can pray for others. We might think that this ministry is not for us, that we are not in the habit of praying for the sick, nor really, if we are honest, do we have much desire to do so. However, almost all of us are actually involved in ministering to those who are sick either by interceding for them, lifting them up before God's throne, or by the many practical ways in which we seek to bring comfort and help to those who are hurting. This final section opens up a way in which we can begin to pray for others and bring them into the presence of the healing Jesus.

In one church, we prayed for a lady. In many ways she was an ordinary person going through the struggles and strains of ordinary life. During ministry time she had a moment when she sensed the presence of Jesus standing just in front of her in such a real way. Afterwards she looked up and said, 'That was a little bit life changing!'

At another church, a young lady had a beautiful sense of Jesus standing right in front of her – it was only afterwards that she discovered that without any prayer being offered, her painful knee condition had been healed at that very moment.

At this point I want to express my gratitude to the many people who have been such an encouragement along the way as I have walked this path of seeking to discover more about Jesus' healing heart. Many won't even know the part they played as they shared their personal experience of meeting with Jesus or asked a particular question at the end of a talk, and yet they have shaped my thinking in some way.

Then there are others who deserve a particular mention. These people may only be names on a page to you but they deserve full credit and my heartfelt thanks for their major contribution to this book.

First, I want to thank the wonderful staff at CHM (Sarah, Gillian, Liz, Denise and Caroline) for their unwavering support, real willingness to try out new ideas and their constant focus on what God is doing. I am also so grateful to all our volunteers who consistently minister with a selflessness and energy that leaves me amazed.

I also owe an enormous debt to our Trustees who encourage me in everything and let me get away with nothing! My thanks especially to Charles Whitehead for writing the Foreword to this book, which has made even me want to read the book all over again.

Finally, I could not do anything without the ongoing patience and wisdom of my wife Gillian, who has been a constant well-spring of encouragement as together we have sought to introduce this approach to healing to churches and groups up and down the country.

John Ryeland

PART

1

**DISCOVERING
WHO WE ARE**

1
WHO DO YOU THINK YOU ARE?

One of the issues we must face whenever we begin to think about prayer, healing or intimacy with God is whether we believe these things are actually for us, or are they for special people who seem to be set aside from birth for a close relationship with Jesus?

We have all met people who seem to have had amazing encounters with God, or whose lives have been so dramatically changed and turned around that it seems obvious they are destined for great things with him. Such stories are wonderful, but they can leave us thinking that we're just ordinary, perhaps more in God's 'B' team than in his Olympic squad. Such thinking is so far from the truth – every one of us is so special to him. To illustrate this, I would like to share something of my own story with God.

My story actually starts before I was born. It goes back to before the creation of the world. Way back then, God looked over all that was to be in the time that was to come, and because I was to be unique he knew the exact moment he would place me in creation and the precise location. It is almost unbelievable, but millions of years before my birth he knew the time when he would bring me into his world.

The reason he did this was not because of anything I would achieve in my lifetime, but simply because he loved me and he made a choice that he was going to pour out on me exactly the same love that he had for his Son, Jesus. Having that love for me, he held me in it and when the time was right, God caused me to be born in exactly the right time and place he had determined for me, such was the value he put on me.

Deciding to leave nothing to chance, two thousand years before I was born, God did something that was to dramatically change the life I was to lead all those years later – he gave his Son, Jesus, who died for me, and in that act of death God made provision for the forgiveness of all my sin. It is as if my sins were Jesus' sins, and his righteousness and cleanness became my righteousness and cleanness. Knowing that I would be able to experience the Father's love as much as he did, Jesus chose to suffer untold agony so that nothing would come between me and the Father, who has planned such love for me. As soon as I was born, God started drawing me towards himself, longing for the time when I would respond and he would live in me through his Holy Spirit. By doing this, he made his very home in me. That is how close God wants to be to me.

Each of us is loved and cherished by God in a way that is so special and unique

From that moment, there was not a single second when I have been alone, not a single moment when the presence of God has not been as close to me as the air that I breathe. Whenever I wandered away, he beckoned me back, and he longs for the day when we will be fully united and I will be able to look back and see the wonder of his guiding hand throughout my life.

That is my story; it is also your story. It is the story of every Christian who has ever lived and will live. Each of us is loved and cherished by God in a way that is so special and unique. This book is an attempt to encourage us to find the reality of that love for ourselves, and discover what happens when we seek to pass it on to other people.

2
GOD'S HEART REVEALED

At the heart of what I have been discovering about healing and about prayer is the truth that our Father longs to meet with us through the person of Jesus, and that we can have an encounter with Jesus that can become a daily reality for us.

However, the very thought of 'encountering' Jesus may seem threatening. Do you want to be that close to God? What will happen? What might he say to you? What might he do? It is probably true that our confidence in being able to answer these questions will depend on our willingness to seek to discover his presence – after all, if we believe that God is seeking us in order to punish us, we are hardly likely to run with any great enthusiasm towards him!

. . . our Father longs to meet with us through the person of Jesus

So many people are under the misapprehension that God has a real desire to punish us. We may feel he has been watching all the wrong things we have been doing in our lives and recording them all in some large black book. The fear is that either in this life or in the next – or probably both – he will throw the book at us. Or it may be that if we are going through a time of particular difficulty, perhaps that sense of punishment is exactly what we may feel he wants to inflict, that we are reaping the just desserts of all our actions. If we feel like that, standing before God does sound like a very risky business indeed.

To begin to understand something of how God really sees us, we need to turn to a passage that may be familiar, as it forms the basis for the blessing that closes many church services. Far from being just a general blessing of kind words, it is a beautiful revelation of God's heart for us:

The LORD bless you and keep you;
the LORD make his face shine on you and be gracious to you;
the LORD turn his face towards you and give you peace.
(Numbers 6:24–26)

'The LORD bless you . . .'

We may genuinely believe that if God were to write a report about us, the very best we could hope for would be along the lines of 'could do better'! Yet in this passage the first words God wants spoken over his people are good words – 'The Lord bless you'. We can relax, God is not going to say anything bad over us and neither will he reveal our sins; his heart's desire is for good things to happen to his people. The word 'bless' is a powerful one: when the Hebrew Bible was translated into Greek, the word chosen for 'bless' was *eulogio* which means 'to speak well of'. That same Greek word for 'bless' is used throughout the New Testament, too. So at the heart of this phrase is the idea that God thinks well of us, speaks well of us and acts in a kind manner towards us.

'. . . and keep you'

The next part of the blessing is the word 'keep'. This word conveys the sense that God is watching, or paying attention, not in the sense of watching to see what we will do wrong, but rather watching with a view to preserve and protect, or guard, us. Why would God want to guard that of which he disapproves? He guards what he believes to be valuable and of worth.

'the Lord make his face shine on you . . .
the Lord turn his face towards you . . .'

These next two phrases are very similar. They are both beautiful phrases, and are almost identical in the Hebrew translation, with only one word being different. The literal translations of these phrases don't make obvious sense in English, but they are something like this: 'The Lord his face to you, shine', and 'The Lord his face to you, lift'. Let's first look at the notion of the face of God – what does 'face' mean here? Are we meant to understand it as we would understand the face of a friend or family member? Probably not! In Exodus 33, we read in verse 11 that 'The Lord would speak to Moses face to face.'

The initial impression given here is that God and Moses would sit together in a very tangible way and talk. Yet just a few verses further on in verse 20, God says to Moses, 'You cannot see my face, for no one may see me and live.'

In other words, the face-to-face conversations that Moses would have with God were not of a visible nature, but were nonetheless intimate and personal. This is not a situation that was meant to be unique to Moses, however. In a number of instances in the Old Testament there are encouragements to seek the face of God:

Seek his face always. (1 Chronicles 16:11)

My heart says of you, 'Seek his face!' Your face, Lord, I will seek. (Psalm 27:8)

In the light of what God says about the impossibility of seeing his face lest we die, this encouragement seems to be more about actively pursuing his presence than trying to look into his face.

We may wonder whether we need to make such an effort. After all, do we not know his presence through the Holy Spirit who lives within us? Interestingly, the New Testament offers similar encouragement although the language is slightly different. Hebrews 10:22 encourages us to 'Draw near to God'.

These words were addressed to followers who already had a hope in Christ. Similarly, James encouraged the Christians to whom he was writing to 'Come near to God and he will come near to you' (James 4:8).

However much we have the Holy Spirit within us, both the Old and New Testaments encourage us to make the effort to seek God's presence and enjoy a closeness with him.

So the idea of the Lord's face being 'turned' or 'lifted' towards us seems to be a reference to the sense of favour or pleasure he has in us. If the face of God was turned away or turned down, that would signify his displeasure towards us. Deuteronomy 31:17 speaks of God hiding his face in anger, and in Psalm 30:7 the psalmist is dismayed because the Lord's face is hidden. These instances of the Lord's face being hidden are specific references to particular circumstances rather than his general attitude towards us.

Secondly, what does the shining face of God signify? In Psalm 80, there appear to be three references to this phrase:

Make your face shine on us, that we may be saved.
(verses 3, 7 and 19)

Reading this psalm, we learn that the writer is distraught at the conditions under which the people of God are living so he calls out for God to make his face shine upon them, not just so they will have a warm, inner cosiness, but so that it might have a direct effect upon their situation – in other words, that they may be saved. This salvation is linked closely to the final part of the blessing, namely that God would give us peace.

'. . . and give you peace'

When Isaiah looked forward to the ministry of the coming Messiah, one of the titles he foresaw being given to the Messiah was that of the Prince of Peace (Isaiah 9:6). We tend to think of peace as a concept, like the absence of war or a storm. In the Bible, however, it carries a much greater and more positive sense, and is linked in with the message of Jesus. When Jesus spoke about the gift of peace that he came to bring, he deliberately

> . . . in his ministry . . . peace to the sinner was forgiveness; peace to the broken was restoration; and peace to the sick was healing

spoke about it being very different from our understanding and experience of peace. He said, 'Peace I leave with you; my peace I give you. I do not give to you as the world gives' (John 14:27).

Jesus meant that the peace he gives is different from what anyone else can give, and this is what we see him demonstrating in his ministry during his lifetime: peace to the sinner was forgiveness; peace to the broken was restoration; and peace to the sick was healing. This was the ministry of the Prince of Peace then, and it is still his ministry now. In the New Testament, the word 'salvation' applies to different situations, including salvation from our sins, deliverance from spirits (Luke 8:36) and healing (Mark 5:28 – the word translated as 'healed' is the Greek word 'saved', as in Mark 10:52 and Acts 4:9).

This blessing confirms that God's attitude towards us is one of pleasure. Does this mean that God approves of everything that we do? Certainly not, but this is what his ministry to us is all about: he wants to bring help, healing and his peace to those parts of our lives that are not yet at peace. It is all too easy to equate this desire of God's with a sense of his displeasure at us, but actually it is his love calling us to see our lives from a different perspective.

> *We were in a church, leading people into an encounter with Jesus. Afterwards, someone shared what had happened to them. For many years they had lived with the fear that they had failed God because of something that had not gone well, and for all that time they had sought the Lord's forgiveness. During the encounter, their perspective had been totally changed when Jesus spoke and told them that they had not failed him at all, it was simply that the timing had not been right.*

For some of us, it is not so much a sense of God's displeasure that troubles us, but rather a fear of divine amnesia: has God forgotten me? We may think that God is not actually against us, but simply that we are somewhere in the crowds getting on with life in an ordinary way. Our sense is that we will probably never do anything extraordinary for God, and he will probably not do anything extraordinary for us. We will carry on in genial co-existence for the rest of our lives. The underlying thought that consumes us is that we are not really that special in the eyes of God; there is nothing wrong with us, but there is nothing extraordinary about us either. However, nothing could be further from the truth. If we can accept this simple blessing as a message from God's heart to ours, we can begin to rest in his love and pleasure.

3
SPEAKING HIS BLESSING OVER US

One of the great challenges that we face in our faith is being able to take the truths of which the Bible speaks and apply them to ourselves. At several points throughout this book, there will be times when you can put these truths into practice. At the heart of this is worship. Worship, first and foremost, is not about what we sing, but rather is about being open to the wonder of God and letting that appreciation of him change us.

For example, we can take each phrase of the blessing in Numbers 6:24–26 and turn it into a phrase of worship to God. The more we can put this into our own words, the more personal it will be. You might want to think along these lines, starting with the opening phrase, 'The LORD bless you':

Lord, I worship you whose heart's desire is to bless me.

I am sorry for those times when I see you as a punishing and unforgiving God.

I am sorry that I miss the love you have for me.

I worship you whose nature is to bless, to think well of me and to speak well of me.

Take each phrase of this blessing and turn it into a time of your own personal worship to God.

The LORD bless you and keep you;

the LORD make his face shine on you and be gracious to you;

the LORD turn his face towards you and give you peace.

4
FOUR TRUTHS FROM EPHESIANS 1

Ephesians 1 directly challenges the way we think about ourselves. In this chapter, Paul shares with us something of how God sees us. He doesn't write in terms of an 'A' team and a 'B' team, but rather these are truths that are applicable to all of us.

Most people will probably read these truths and ignore them on the basis that they are far too good to be believable. That is why they are written down for us; we can keep coming back to them and see them as truths that are directly applicable to us. If you read these truths and doubt their application to you – that somehow these words only apply to some Christians and not to others (and we always tend to put ourselves in the category of 'others'!) – a more appropriate reaction is to say 'yes' to each of these words and choose to see that they apply to you personally.

It might seem rather obvious, but Ephesians 1 is the first chapter in Paul's letter to the Ephesians. In other words, it must be read and digested before the rest of the letter. All too often, we read the passages about the ways in which we should behave and the 'armour of God' without really taking to heart the wonders of the first chapter. Ephesians 1 is a chapter that provides us with the foundations upon which we are meant to build our lives. Unless we are doing this, then it is a fair question to ask what our foundations are.

Within this chapter, Paul highlights four words, each of which is both a general truth for every one of us, but also uniquely applicable to us, as if we were the only person in the world.

1. Chosen

The first word is *chosen* (Ephesians 1:4).

A common experience for many people is that they sense rejection, either by family, friends or other people who let them down. If we are tempted to dwell on a sense of rejection, this word 'chosen' is such a beautiful stamp upon us, that no matter what opinion the world or other people may have of us, the Lord God, creator of heaven and earth, has chosen us.

A common reason as to why people doubt they are chosen is because they can see no earthly reason why God would possibly choose them. They haven't done anything particularly good, they have just been getting on and working out their life with God. There is, however, a beautiful detail in this verse: when Paul says that we were chosen 'before the creation of the world', he means

. . . no matter what opinion the world or other people may have of us, the Lord God, creator of heaven and earth, has chosen us

that God's choice was not made on the basis of our achievements or past record.

When I was at school, the common system for deciding who would play on which sports team was for each captain to select, one by one, those they would choose to join their team. Naturally, their decisions in making their selections were based on their peers' past performances and skills. This is a natural way of making human choices. We look at the options and make our choices appropriately from the information we have. If God were to make his choices on this basis, we might have reason to doubt whether we would be chosen, but what Ephesians says is that this is precisely how God does *not* make choices. He chose us before the creation of the world, before we were born, before we did anything good or bad. A natural reaction is, 'Why? Why would God do that?' The next word gives us a clue.

2. Adopted

We are also *adopted* (Ephesians 1:5). What the verse actually says is that 'in love he predestined us to be adopted'. The word 'predestination' may be enough to set us into a spin. What if I wasn't predestined? What if I think I am a Christian, but God never actually predestined me for this?

We are looking at this issue from the wrong perspective if we think of predestination in terms of who is predestined and who is not. Perhaps a better way of looking at predestination is, as Paul puts it in Ephesians 1, not *who* is predestined, but rather *what* it is to which we are predestined. In other words, the Father decided before he created the world that he would adopt us as his own beloved children. Nothing can now change that decision. This truth becomes important when we have moments of feeling that we must be such a disappointment to God that he somehow wants to un-adopt us. The way Paul puts it is that this concept would be unthinkable to God. This has already been hinted at in a passage from Isaiah: 'Can a mother forget the baby at her breast and have no compassion on the child she has borne? Though she may forget, I will not forget you!' (Isaiah 49:15). What God is communicating to us here is that even if a human mother could forget her child, it would be unthinkable for him to do so with us. We have been predestined for adoption; there is no other relationship God has in store for us.

Alternatively, we may think of ourselves as God's distant relatives and that we are lucky if he remembers who we are. This, again, is simply not true – as far as God is concerned, we are his adopted children and he is unfailingly committed to an intimate relationship with us.

In the context of the Roman world in which Paul lived, a Roman parent would select one child – perhaps not even one of his own children – to whom he wanted to pass on his inheritance or his title. He would adopt them so that they could then enjoy a new status as an adopted child. All their previous debts would be cancelled and they would enjoy all the rights and privileges of their new status.

Perhaps one way in which we can better understand adoption is that if a couple already have a child and decide to adopt, they bring the adopted child into their new family and pour out on the adopted child all the love that they have for their existing child. It is not about labelling their children as biological or adopted, they are both fully their children. In this context, the Father adopts us to be children alongside the existing family he has – namely himself and Jesus – so that we might share in their love. In the final verse of John 17 (the whole chapter is a prayer from Jesus to his Father), Jesus shares something very beautiful about his understanding of God's love that we, too, are welcome to experience: 'I have made you known to them, and will continue to make you known in order that the love you have for me may be in them' (John 17:26). In this verse, Jesus also reveals that everything he had been doing was actually a revelation of his Father; all his teaching and miracles were intended to show us just what the Father is really like. The reason for this revelation is not just so we can have a clearer picture of God but, as Jesus explains in verse 26, so that 'the love you [Father] have for me [Jesus] may be in them [all of us]'. In other words, Jesus' desire is that we share in the love he and his Father share.

At one of our teaching days, a lady shared what she sensed as she met with Jesus. Jesus was on her right with his arm round her, and she felt the same on her left. She knew she was in the presence of the Father, but was hiding behind Jesus. He then moved in front of her and behind so that he made the shape of the cross all around her. Jesus said to her, 'When the Father looks at you, he thinks it's me.'

A second way in which we can understand the concept of adoption is in terms of 're-parenting'. As children we may well have had a less than perfect experience of being brought up by our parents. Such experiences can create negative reactions to the concept of 'Father God' and we may relate the word 'Father' to what we experienced in childhood. The adopting God changes that; he gives us a new vision of fatherhood. Going back to Jesus' phrase in John 17:26, 'I have made you known to them, and will continue to make you known', what is meant here is that throughout Jesus' ministry, and in the events of the passion that were about to unfold, he revealed the Father to us so that no one can say that they do not know what our Father God is like. Jesus told the disciples something similar when he stated in John 14:9 that 'Anyone who has seen me has seen the Father.' When Jesus healed the sick, and when he forgave sinners, he was reflecting the wonderful heart of our Father.

When Jesus healed the sick, and when he forgave sinners, he was reflecting the wonderful heart of our Father

3. Forgiven

The third word that Paul uses in Ephesians 1 is the word *forgiven* (Ephesians 1:7). Forgiveness is God's choice to reach out to what is sinful in our lives, to take it from us and place it upon Jesus. From this point it is no longer something we bear, but something that is upon him. It is not that God ignores our sin or sweeps it under the carpet, but rather that he deals with it by forgiveness. Forgiveness should never be approached purely as a concept, and we should seek to allow the truth of it to amaze us at every opportunity.

Many people view forgiveness in terms of a filing cabinet, in that when we confess our sins they are taken off God's desk and out of his immediate gaze, and filed away in some enormous divine filing cabinet alongside all the other sins we have committed and confessed. Every time we confess another sin, it is added to an ever-growing folder. A better analogy of what happens to our sin is that of a shredder. Once we confess that sin, it is gone – shredded – and cannot be retrieved. It really is **Forgiveness should never be approached purely as a concept, and we should seek to allow the truth of it to amaze us at every opportunity** as the letter to the Hebrews states: 'Their sins and lawless acts I will remember no more' (Hebrews 10:17). Another good analogy is of writing the word 'paid' on a bill when we pay it, in the sure knowledge that the bill is dealt with and can never be presented to us again. The bill has not been ignored, and neither have we been let off the consequences of having a bill, but rather it is paid for in full. Of course, where these analogies fall down is that while it costs us nothing to file something, feed a piece of paper through a shredder or stamp 'paid' on a bill, it cost Jesus everything to take our sin upon himself.

It is worth reflecting on why God would go to those lengths for us. We often think of this in terms of the benefit to us. Jesus died for us so that we can be free and face the future without the weight of our sins around our neck. However, forgiveness is something God does for his benefit as well as for ours. The serious nature of sin means it cannot simply be disregarded, and without some effective way of dealing with it, sin will separate God from us so that he is unable to enjoy the relationship he so desperately wants with us. What Jesus did on the cross is an act that both deals with sin and blesses the Father; God is now able to embrace us without the barrier of sin dividing us.

. . . forgiveness is something God does for his benefit as well as for ours

There are two aspects to our coming to God to seek forgiveness. When we come to God, whether by way of a dramatic conversion or by a gradual process over a period of time, he takes from us all that stands against us, as if taking off dirty clothes and dressing us in new clothing, so that we stand before him as forgiven people. God has always loved us, but because of the forgiveness we accept from him, he is able to come to us in a way that he could not before. As part of our on-going process of transformation, it is a wonderful discipline to spend some time reflecting on each day as it ends, giving thanks for what has been good, confessing what we feel it would be right to confess, and forgiving those who have caused offence to us. We are not endlessly confessing the same sins, as what is the point when he remembers our sins no more? However, our confession may reveal habits and patterns that need his transformative touch.

The New Testament makes it clear that as wonderful as it is to be forgiven by God, there is a calling upon us to be forgiving people as well as forgiven people. Paul writes a little later on in Ephesians, 'Be kind and compassionate to one another, forgiving each other, just as in Christ God forgave you. Follow God's example' (Ephesians 4:32 – 5:1). By undertaking to pass on forgiveness as freely as we have received it, Paul says that we actually begin to imitate God and to share in his nature in a wonderful way.

One young person who has been coming to our Mission shared her story about what happened to her in a particular church service, and how she was led to forgive her own father in a powerful way:

'One day, I was coming to church and my hands were cold. The next minute they were warm. Jesus turned round to me and said, "That's because my hands were on yours." They went warm in the end. He looked at me and said, "Do you love me and have trust and faith in me?" And I said, "Yes." So he said, "When you're ready to forgive your dad, just hold my hand and I will be here for you and then you leave him to me." That's when I said I wanted to forgive my dad. He said "Are you ready now?" I took his hand. I said, "I forgive him." He couldn't pick me up quick enough. He swung me round and said, "I'm so proud of you!" He had a sparkle in his eye and cried, then said, "You can do it when you put your mind to it and just relax!" He cuddled me, kissed me, and said, "I love you my child."'

4. Marked

The fourth word that Paul uses to describe us in Ephesians 1 is the word *marked*. In verse 13 it says, 'You were marked in him with a seal, the promised Holy Spirit.' This is something to which we shall return later when we consider our vision of ourselves, but at this point what it means for us to be marked is that we take seriously Paul's statement in 1 Corinthians 6:19 that we are temples of the Holy Spirit. Our physical bodies are physical dwelling places of his presence.

To be marked is to bear the name of God

As we have been discovering, although we may tend to think of ourselves as worthless, we are far more highly valued in God's sight than we can ever imagine. This is not simply about how we view ourselves; it is about our identity – who we actually are. In 1 Corinthians 6:19 Paul writes, 'Do you not know that your bodies are temples of the Holy Spirit, who is in you, whom you have received from God?' The context of this passage is actually a warning for Christians not to indulge in immorality, because our physical bodies are special places in which God has placed his Holy Spirit. However, the implications of what Paul says actually go beyond this warning and say something wonderful about who we are.

Let us look again at this verse a little more closely:

'Do you not know . . .'
The implication of this phrase is that Paul was about to remind his readers of something they should have been well aware of, and which also applies to every one of us.

'. . . that your bodies are temples of the Holy Spirit . . .'
This is evocative language: a temple was not just any old building, it was specifically constructed with one purpose in mind, namely that it would be set apart as a sacred place.

'. . . who is in you . . .'
Paul is not addressing just one or two people who may have had a mystical spiritual experience; he is talking to everyone who will hear or receive his letter. This is a truth for all of us and every one of us can apply this truth as a reality for us personally.

'. . . whom you have received from God?'
The point about this phrase is that it is not about us or whether we have done enough to qualify for this privilege of being temples of the Holy Spirit. This is something that God has decided to do, and has done by his action and initiative.

So the question 'What does God think of me?' is summed up beautifully in Ephesians 1. It's not about how we see ourselves – even if we consider ourselves as bruised and battered or as failures – but how God sees us as people who are chosen, people who have been adopted, people who are forgiven and people who are marked with the very presence of his Spirit. That's what God thinks of us. That is his heart for us.

The reality is that we think so little of ourselves. We are all too aware of our weaknesses and our failures and know only too well the damage that can be done to us by other people's words and attitudes. What we need to catch is the wonder of who we are, which the Bible reveals.

5
MAKING THE TRUTH REAL TO US

I often find myself holding a cross in my hands as I pray. One reason is that simply touching a cross is a tangible way of keeping my concentration fixed on what I am doing. Another reason is that holding different parts of the cross at various moments helps me to pause on the particular issue about which I am seeking to concentrate.

It might be helpful to hold a cross to ponder these four glorious truths in Ephesians 1. Hold onto each of the four 'arms' of the cross in turn and take time to worship God for the truth of each of these specific words. The very act of holding onto or touching a different 'arm' for each of these words will help to slow your thoughts down so that you can consciously dwell on each particular word.

Hold one of the 'arms' of the cross and worship God. Acknowledge that it is true you are personally chosen. The less you believe it to be true of yourself, the more time you may need to spend on this particular truth.

The more personal you can make it, the better, but it might be helpful to begin along these lines:

I worship you, Father, and thank you that you have chosen me.

You chose me before the foundation of the world.

Before I did one good thing, you chose me.

I worship you because you still choose me.

You promised never to reject me.

Carry on until some of this truth begins to touch you deeply. When you feel it is appropriate, move your fingers to another 'arm' of the cross and begin to worship him for the truth that he has adopted you. Then move on in the same way to dwell on his forgiveness, and the fact that you are marked with his presence.

6
BEING A NAME-BEARER

The implication of being a temple of the Holy Spirit is enormous: we carry within us something of the actual presence of God.

After Solomon constructed the Temple in 2 Chronicles, he dedicated it to God and set out his dream for it. In reply to his prayer, we read that fire came down from heaven and God appeared to him and revealed something of his vision for the Temple: 'Now my eyes will be open and my ears attentive to the prayers offered in this place. I have chosen and consecrated this temple so that my Name may be there for ever. My eyes and my heart will always be there' (2 Chronicles 7:15–16).

. . . we carry within us something of the actual presence of God

The presence of God within the Temple is summed up by the use of the word 'Name'. When the Bible speaks of the name of God, it means more than what we might understand by that word. We use a person's name to call them or to identify them, but in the Bible the name of God is more than how we address him, it is to do with representing all that he is. Jeremiah takes this concept a stage further. In Jeremiah 15:16, we read these words: 'I bear your name, LORD God Almighty.' So not only does a temple bear the name of God, we do too. If we take seriously the fact that God can dwell within us, what is the nature of God like exactly?

There are several occasions in the Old Testament when people discovered something new about the nature of God, and as a result of their experience they built a memorial and named that place as a reminder of what they had learned about his nature. These revelations were laid down as markers for future generations to remember so that the stunning nature of what they experienced becomes our experience; we can count their life-changing discovery as being equally true for us without having to go through the same process. We do not have to repeat what Abraham went through, for example, to have permission to live in the truth that God is our provider and to allow that revelation to be a foundation for our own lives. Let's take a look at some of these names, or truths, that we can sow into our lives as name-bearers.

Being Marked with the Name of the Provider

The first name for God can be found in Genesis 22. In this passage we find Abraham facing his hardest test. The background to this story is that for years Abraham had been promised a son through whom he would have countless descendants. Eventually the promise was fulfilled and Abraham and Sarah had their son, Isaac. In Genesis 22, Abraham is asked to face the ultimate test, in that he is asked to sacrifice their son to God. The story is well known; at the last minute God provides a ram for Abraham to sacrifice in place of Isaac. In verse 14 we read: 'Abraham called that place The LORD Will Provide.' Whenever Abraham went back to that place in his mind, he was reminded of the truth he discovered that God would always be his provider. That phrase reflects a truth about God that Abraham would have carried with him for the rest of his life.

This is an aspect of God's character that we also carry with us wherever we go. We hold on to this truth not only for our own blessing, but as something that we can carry to others. In many ways it sums up other characteristics of God – he is the one who provides both for our needs and for the needs of others.

Being Marked with the Name of the Banner

Another name is that of 'banner'. This comes from Exodus 17, where Moses is standing on a hill watching Joshua fight with the Amalekites in the valley below. Moses holds his staff in his hands and when he raises his arms Joshua begins to gain the victory. When Moses lowers his arms Joshua begins to suffer defeat. Moses' assistants then sit him down and help him by holding his arms up so that victory is assured. After Joshua wins the battle, Moses builds an altar and calls the place 'The LORD is my Banner'.

The application of this story for us is that when we hold up the wonder of Jesus, we will begin to see victory. Like Moses, we also carry something, but it is a cross rather than a staff. When Moses felt the staff in his hands, it must have filled him with great confidence. It was this staff that he had seen turn into a snake, and the same staff with which he had struck the ground and seen the dust turn to a swarm of gnats. Moses had even used this staff to part the Red Sea for the Israelites to pass through after their escape from Egypt. Just to hold his staff must have been a constant reminder to Moses of the power of God and the possibility of what God could do.

Mentally holding onto the image of the cross can have a similar effect for us. The cross is the supreme reminder of the love that Jesus has for us, a love so strong that he was willing to lay down his life for us so that we might experience the fullness of life that he came to bring. It was on the cross that Jesus paid for the sins of the world – our own sins, and those of every person with whom we come into contact. It was on the cross that Jesus disarmed the powers of the enemy, so that the victory over evil might be complete. It was on the cross that our sinful natures were crucified with him so that we might live a life that is as new as the risen life of Jesus. As we go about our daily lives, we carry with us the reality of what Jesus has done. In bearing his name, we carry the banner of God's victory with us. It is not too much of an exaggeration to say that

> In bearing his name, we carry the banner of God's victory with us

wherever we walk, we carry into every place and situation the truth of what Jesus did by dying on the cross for us. We are now changed, forgiven people because of that one event, and we carry that change and forgiveness with us wherever we go.

Being Marked with Peace

Another beautiful aspect of God's nature that we carry with us is something that Gideon discovered and noted in Judges 6. In verse 24 Gideon calls the place where he makes this discovery, 'The LORD Is Peace'. God had appeared to Gideon, apparently in the form of an angel, but Gideon knew enough to realise that to see God was to die, because that was the revelation God had given Moses in Exodus 33:20 ('No one may see me and live'). Having just had this revelation of God, Gideon is naturally fearful, but he is immediately reassured that he is not going to die. In his relief and gratitude, he calls the place of his discovery 'The LORD Is Peace'.

Fear is very much around us. The reason for our fears may be varied, but into every aspect of fear we carry this amazing presence of God, namely that the Lord is peace. He is not angry with us, rather he has demonstrated the lengths to which he will go to show his love, compassion and commitment to us by allowing

Jesus to willingly give himself up to die. Whatever we feel may disqualify us from being in the presence of God, whatever there may be from our pasts that causes fear to fill us, the truth that Gideon discovered stands also for us – the Lord is our peace.

Being Marked with Righteousness

At other points in the Bible, rather than people marking the place where they make a discovery about God, they note something that God speaks about himself. An example of this is in Jeremiah 23:6 where the prophet records God's declaration, 'This is the name by which he will be called: The LORD Our Righteous Saviour.'

The name 'righteous' reminds us that we can know freedom from whatever we feel we may have done wrong in our lives and is holding us back. Jesus has paid the price for our sins and as a consequence of his actions we no longer need to feel disqualified by our own mistakes. It is not that our sins have been swept under the carpet, or that they did not matter, but rather that they have been dealt with. We can therefore go into any situation with the firm conviction that we stand before God and before others with a clean heart. He can and will use us, because we carry with us the truth that the living Lord God has declared us clean.

. . . we carry with us the truth that the living Lord God has declared us clean

Being Marked with the Name of the Healer

One more noteworthy name of God that we bear is that of the Lord who heals us (Exodus 15:26). The circumstances behind the giving of this name were the Israelites grumbling about the lack of water in the desert, as the water where they were camped was too bitter to drink. Through a miracle the water became drinkable, and then God promised that if his people would stay loyal to him, he would prevent disease among them because he is the one who heals.

A few things are worth mentioning about this name for God. What is of interest is that this, too, is a name given by God. This is not simply a description that people arrived at through experience, but it is one that God has deliberately revealed about himself. The second element to note about this revelation is that it is about change. God does not reveal himself here as the one who simply cares or sympathises, but as the one who brings change, transformation and protection.

Healing can be quite a difficult word to define. We often hear it spoken of in terms of 'wholeness'. Perhaps it can be thought of in terms of a touch of God by which we become the people that God created us to be. The New Testament contains many stories of healing, for example blind Bartimaeus receiving his sight, where the change that Jesus brings is physical and dramatic. However, there are other stories of transformation that

> **God does . . . reveal himself here as the one . . . who brings change, transformation and protection**

aren't about physical change. One such story occurs in John 21, where Jesus asked Peter a similar question three times. As the disciples met with the risen Jesus, Peter was probably waiting anxiously for something to be said to him about the way in which he had denied Jesus three times, but the manner in which Jesus addressed him was totally affirming, life giving and transforming.

A question we need to ask is this: if God has revealed himself as the one who heals, does this mean he always promises healing on every occasion when we pray? Paul wrote this about the promises of God:

No matter how many promises God has made, they are 'Yes' in Christ. (2 Corinthians 1:20)

What Paul is saying here is that the nature of God's promises is different now than it was then; the person of Jesus has made a difference. In other words, promises usually came with a condition in the Old Testament. The promise in Exodus, whereby God reveals himself as a healer, is no exception. The revelation of God as healer is prefaced with this condition:

If you listen carefully to the LORD your God and do what is right in his eyes, if you pay attention to his commands and keep all his decrees, I will not bring on you any of the diseases I brought on the Egyptians, for I am the LORD, who heals you. (Exodus 15:26)

When this promise was given, it was not a matter of everyone automatically being healed; it was given on the condition of obedience. If the people were obedient to God, he would heal their diseases. What Paul teaches is that God's promises are not now conditional on obedience, but are released through the ministry of Jesus. It is interesting that when Jesus healed the sick in his ministry, he never put conditions upon them for their healing. One example of this is the story of the ten lepers in Luke 17. We have no indication of who these men were, or of what their relationship with God was like. What we do know is that the tenth leper, who comes back and falls at the feet of Jesus and worships him after his healing, was a Samaritan, considered to be a foreigner. It was not worship to God that released this healing – that response came afterwards. No condition was put on this wonderful thing that Jesus did for them. In John 5, Jesus healed a man who had been unable to walk for the past 38 years. We read in verse 14 that Jesus met the man again and encouraged him to 'stop sinning'. We have no idea what the sin was, but it is interesting that the man's healing was not dependent upon him confessing his sins first. Jesus touched him first and then went on to speak to him about how he was living his life. Healing happens, but it cannot be tied down to just a simple definition of a physical cure. Healing is about God's transformation of every part of us and it is quite conceivable that God's agenda for our transformation may be different from ours. However, this is not to water down the stunning truth that we carry within us the name and the promise of the healing God, the one who came in Jesus to transform us.

It is also worth bearing in mind the truth that this is not simply something that we carry for our own benefit. Carrying the name and the presence of God with us wherever we go means that there is no situation in which we find ourselves, and no person to whom we speak, who cannot be changed by the fact that we carry the presence of God within us. When people meet us they encounter our external identity, but they also meet everything that exists within us. They meet God, who is the provider, the healer and their peace. In fact, Paul writes in two places that our lives are not our own but should be lived for him. He writes in Romans 14:7–8, 'None of us lives for ourselves alone . . . If we live, we live for the Lord.' Similarly, in 2 Corinthians 5:15, 'He died for all, that those who live should no longer live for themselves but for him who died for them and was raised again.'

7
PRACTISING BEING A NAME-BEARER

All these different names for God, revealed in the Bible, stand as promises to us. Each says something about the nature of God in relation to us. Follow this exercise to deepen your awareness of the wonder of God who dwells within you, and the implications of that for you and those with whom you will come into contact.

The exercise is simply to meditate on the words from Jeremiah 15:16: *'I bear your name, LORD God Almighty.'*

- Find a quiet place to sit comfortably without any other distractions around you.

- As you slowly breathe in, let your breathing be accompanied by the words, *'I bear your name'*.

- As you slowly breathe out, concentrate on the words *'Lord God Almighty'*.

- Keep the pattern going for five minutes or longer if you want.

As you do this, it might be helpful to let the day ahead of you play through your mind, pondering the people you expect to meet, the places you will go and the events you have planned. As you run through these scenarios with the words of this phrase going through your mind, what you are doing is bringing each of these people and events into the awareness of the presence of God within you. It is not just that he will accompany you throughout the day, but that people will be actively meeting the presence of God through you.

If you practise this exercise at the end of the day, use the events that have just passed as your focus, recognising God's presence with you even when you may not have been aware of it.

As this practice becomes more natural and familiar, this phrase will begin to run through your mind at other times of the day when you are not consciously praying, bringing a reminder of who you really are and what you carry within you.

This awareness of God within us can really make a difference. All of us need the grace of his presence in our lives. It may be that we have a difficult decision to make, or that we feel led to give something of ourselves beyond our natural abilities or resources. If we can begin by calling to mind the truth that we carry within us the name of the Lord God Almighty, our confidence and expectation is going to increase with the knowledge that it is not just us doing what we can, but God in us. It is also a daily reminder of a truth we so often forget, that we carry his presence with us wherever we go.

PART

2

**MEETING JESUS
IN ENCOUNTER
PRAYER**

8
IT'S ALL ABOUT THE ENCOUNTER

It is very tempting to look at prayer and see it through the lens of 'results'. In other words, if prayer is answered then it must be a good prayer, and if prayer is unanswered, we obviously have some work to do. There are two wonderful stories in the same chapter of the Bible that, when we take them together, show something amazing about prayer, namely that the fact Jesus grants a prayer request is no indication of what he thinks about a situation. This suggests that although our prayers may be answered, this is no barometer of the state of our hearts.

Read these two stories:

Then he got into the boat and his disciples followed him. Suddenly a furious storm came up on the lake, so that the waves swept over the boat. But Jesus was sleeping. The disciples went and woke him, saying, 'Lord, save us! We're going to drown!' He replied, 'You of little faith, why are you so afraid?' Then he got up and rebuked the winds and the waves, and it was completely calm. (Matthew 8:23–26)

When Jesus had entered Capernaum, a centurion came to him, asking for help. 'Lord,' he said, 'my servant lies at home paralysed, suffering terribly.' Jesus said to him, 'Shall I come and heal him?' The centurion replied, 'Lord, I do not deserve to have you come under my roof. But just say the word, and my servant will be healed. For I myself am a man under authority, with soldiers under me. I tell this one, "Go," and he goes; and that one, "Come," and he comes. I say to my servant, "Do this," and he does it.' When Jesus heard this, he was amazed and said to those following him, 'Truly I tell you, I have not found anyone in Israel with such great faith . . .' Then Jesus said to the centurion, 'Go! Let it be done just as you believed it would.' And his servant was healed at that moment. (Matthew 8:5–13)

Both of these stories contain similar elements. Both involve issues that are brought to Jesus:

● The disciples are afraid for their lives because of the storm.

● The centurion has a servant who is sick.

Both of them bring their requests to Jesus:

● The disciples wake up Jesus, who is sleeping in the boat, and beg for his help.

● The centurion comes to Jesus and asks for help.

Both of them have their prayers answered:

● The storm is stilled.

● The servant is healed.

The difference between the stories is in the reaction of Jesus:

● He calls the disciples faithless.

● He is amazed at the faith of the centurion.

The particular way in which faith seems to be commented on by Jesus is in terms of what each of these people focused on. The disciples were transfixed by the storm – all they could see were the waves becoming higher and higher. The centurion's focus was on the wonder of Jesus. That is why he could see that Jesus did not even need to come into his home; it was enough that Jesus simply spoke a word. The centurion knew power would flow from that word. Jesus called the men focusing on the storm 'faithless', but he was amazed at the man who could see the wonder of who he was. Both these stories are about answered prayer, but I'm certain that we would much rather amaze Jesus for the right reasons, and not because of our faithlessness!

As we come on to look at the question of how we should pray, it is clearly not a matter of simply judging our prayers by whether or not they are answered, but whether our focus is on the right thing – Jesus. One of the easiest things to do when we are praying is to put our focus immediately on the issue that is looming large in front of us – there it is, demanding our attention, and it doesn't seem to want to go away; it seems only natural to give it our total and immediate focus. However, by falling into this pattern of thinking it is all too easy for us to forget the simple step of first coming to Jesus. Prayer is not simply a matter of speaking about something to God, it is about bringing something into the relationship we have with Jesus, and that is what we are going to focus on in this section: how can we increase the reality of our relationship with Jesus?

Encountering Jesus should not be a difficult thing for us. There is a very well-known verse in the book of Revelation that gives us a glimpse into the reality of what life with Jesus should be like: 'Here I am! I stand at the door and knock. If anyone hears my voice and opens the door, I will come in and eat with that person, and they with me' (Revelation 3:20). We are the ones who have heard the voice of Jesus knocking, we have let him in and his promise is, 'I will come in and eat with that person, and they with me.' It is that sense of eating together that is what we miss out on.

It sums up the quality of fellowship and friendship that describes what our relationship with Jesus should be like – it should be like eating with him. That is what Jesus thinks is normal fellowship. Our experience of food is that it should be regular and often! We do not have an enormous meal once a year that is meant to sustain us for the next 365 days. Food should be a regular thing for us and as this is the analogy in the verse from Revelation, why can't our experience of Jesus be of a similar nature? It is not something for special occasions. Paul wrote at the beginning of 1 Corinthians, 'God is faithful, who has called you into fellowship with his Son, Jesus Christ our Lord' (1 Corinthians 1:9). Fellowship is all about an on-going relationship with Jesus – as close as him eating with us. So how can we increase our experience of Jesus?

The first step is to believe that we really can experience him. This is not just something for a selected few – all of us are called into fellowship with Jesus. Fellowship and relationship are part of the normal Christian life. It sounds almost ridiculous to talk about how to have a relationship with Jesus when it is something that is available already. Perhaps what we

Fellowship is all about an on-going relationship with Jesus

are talking about here is how to increase our consciousness of a relationship that is already present. Over the past few years, we have found an approach that can be of immense value in seeking to bring people to a closer awareness of the presence of Jesus. A helpful image is to think in terms of shining three spotlights in turn on either ourselves or the person for whom we are praying. These spotlights represent:

● The Father's love – a focus on the fact that each one of us is loved individually and uniquely by God the Father.

- The presence of Jesus – an acknowledgement that we really can experience his presence here and now today.

- The power of the Holy Spirit – a recognition that we can expect to experience the transformation that he brings.

This focus on each member of the Trinity in turn – Father, Son and Holy Spirit – is an easy way to help us remember these important truths and to keep them at the forefront of our minds.

Father
Son
Spirit

The first step is to dwell on the truth of the Father's love for us.

Jesus is the bringer of the kingdom of God. In Matthew 18:3 Jesus says: 'Truly I tell you, unless you change and become like little children, you will never enter the kingdom of heaven.' This is doubtless to do with recapturing that sense of wonder and dependency on God, but it could also mean that coming as little children means to come in the knowledge of the parenthood of God. A fascinating question is this: who is it that most people pray to? Some people talk to 'Almighty God' or 'Jesus', but most talk to 'Lord' (I suppose on the basis that somebody up there will receive the prayer, and no one will be offended since they are all 'Lord'!). However, Jesus had views on this. In Luke 11:2 we read: 'He said to them, "When you pray, say: 'Father'."' Of course, it is not the case that your prayers will only be answered if you say 'Father' – it's not the same as making a tiny mistake in a long email address which stops the whole thing working! Perhaps, though, when we say 'Father', it actually shifts our prayers on to a whole new wonderful basis of praying out of relationship and not just out of desperation. When we pray to our 'Father', we are invited to stand in that place of love and intimacy, a place that is so important. So often at the back of our minds is the uncertainty of whether he really loves us. Does he love me today? He might have done so yesterday, but does he love me today? Does he know I'm here? We may never say that out loud, but the whisper is there – does he really love us?

The more we can come back to 'Abba, Father' and the wonderful reality of that relationship, the more those lies and fears get swept away. John talks about fear in one of his letters; it could be the fear of anything, but often it is the fear that God does not really love us. In 1 John 4:18, he writes: 'The one who fears is not made perfect in love.' If you are feeling a little fearful, this may sound rather

When we pray to our 'Father', we are invited to stand in that place of love and intimacy . . .

harsh, but John has caught something here – that actually the answer to our fears is to find again the wonder of the love of God that this word 'Father' encapsulates.

The word 'Abba' is the word that a child would use to address his or her father; it is a word that has connotations of trust, love and dependency. However, it is not simply the word of a child. We find that it is a word on the lips of Jesus at a time of great pain in his ministry.

In Mark 14, Jesus is in the garden of Gethsemane. It is quite easy to imagine the pain he was experiencing was something from which he felt quite detached, but as we read the account it is evident his pain is real and deep. We are told in Mark 14:33–34 that 'he began to be deeply distressed and troubled. "My soul is overwhelmed with sorrow to the point of death," he said.' These words give us an insight into the profound nature of the darkness that was beginning to envelop Jesus. What is fascinating is what he does with this darkness. We are told that he went back to the most important relationship he knew – namely that of himself and the Father. He speaks to God in a way that is personal and loving. The exact word he uses in Mark 14:36 is 'Abba' – the intimate word a child would use of their father. It is on this that Jesus falls back when darkness surrounds him. It is into this 'child – Abba' relationship that we are also invited to partake.

In both Galatians 4:6 and Romans 8:15, Paul alludes to a wonderful ministry of the Holy Spirit, where the Spirit is resident within us calling out 'Abba, Father'. By calling out 'Abba' within us, what the Spirit is seeking to do is to encourage us to catch the profound nature of that word in every part of our being so that we can, with trust and sincerity, know the wonder of God as our 'Abba, Father'. The Father of our Lord Jesus Christ is our Father; the intimacy the Father had with Jesus is the same intimacy we can experience with our heavenly Father. At the beginning of John's Gospel, John reflects on Jesus and on our right to be children of the Father: 'Yet to all who did receive him, to those who believed in his name, he gave the right to become children of God' (John 1:12). We have the right to say, 'Abba, Father.' Whatever you have been through, whatever you are going through, you have the right to call him Father. It is such a wonderful privilege.

At this stage, we may well have to close our minds to false images of fatherhood. Often we look at our own fathers and assume that God must be like them. If our experience of fatherhood is a negative one, then our trust in Father God is also diminished.

Actually, to think like that is quite dangerous. What we are doing is building our image of God from earthly building blocks. We are taking what we see around us or what we have experienced and imagining God from our perspective. No earthly father, no matter how good or kind they are, can match up to the wonder of God the Father. Any earthly images of fatherhood are going to fail if we take them as our starting point to build the image of 'Abba, Father'. The best place to begin to form an image of what Father God is like is to look at Jesus. The Bible says of Jesus that he is 'the exact representation of his [God's] being' (Hebrews 1:3). Jesus said of himself, 'Anyone who has seen me has seen the Father' (John 14:9).

During a time of encouraging people to find the Father's love, one lady shared how Jesus was holding her hand, showing acceptance and love. She had never known what it was like to hold her own father's hand so this was so very special.

If you find it hard to grasp the wonder of the Father, begin to read the gospels thoughtfully, passage by passage, asking at the end of each section: if Jesus reflects the Father, what does this passage tell me about the nature of Father God?

The love of God is not something that we should pass over, it isn't something that we 'take as read' or assume that we know all about. Lamentations 3:22–23 says, 'His compassions never fail. They are new every morning.' Every morning, the sense of his love and compassion for us can be met afresh in our hearts. The awareness of the Father's love should be something to which we return on a daily basis, to begin every time of prayer and worship aware of the depth of his love for us, a love that is unfailing and a love that will never leave us. All too often, our sense that

God doesn't love us as much as he perhaps has done in the past is really due to the fact that we have not spent time coming back to that place of love and making it the starting point of our relationship with him.

So meeting Jesus begins with us worshipping the Father, but we often have strange ideas of what worship is about. Worship is not buttering up God so that he will listen to our requests more favourably! Often we find healing services starting with a time of worship – normally because we think that is what we ought to do. An underlying sense can be that unless we start with worship, God will not listen to us so readily. Worship is not about telling God what he already knows. If God is God, he must know that he is all-powerful and majestic. He is well aware of who he is and who we are as well. Nor is it the case that God needs our worship because he feels somewhat insecure, and needs us to keep telling him how wonderful and loving he is. Worship is all about opening up ourselves to the wonder of the truth. God desires worship, not because it makes a difference to him, but because it changes us. The more we can open our hearts to the wonder of his love for us, the more we are changed by the process. As our hearts grow with the knowledge of his love for us, faith rises within us and hope can fill our hearts. We worship for our benefit, not for his. So when we lift our hearts to worship 'Abba, Father', we are seeking to be open and more aware of the intimate love with which he sees and holds us. It is by worship that the truths that we know in our heads become convictions within our hearts. Perhaps the best way in which we can worship 'Abba' is to begin to remember that the Holy Spirit is already speaking that word in

> **God desires worship, not because it makes a difference to him, but because it changes us**

our hearts, and that we are not starting from a position of being unaware of the Father's heart; a sense of awareness is already planted deep within us. So a good way to begin is by letting the very words 'Abba, Father' go through our minds as we begin to acknowledge what 'Abba, Father' means for us.

Father
Son
Spirit

If we were in need, one of the most exciting visions we could have would be to see Jesus walk into the room where we were. There would be something about his physical presence that would lift our faith and cause our expectations to rise. Yet Jesus is not in this world in the same way as he was during his ministry on earth. He knew that things were going to be different, and actually rejoiced in it. He spoke these words about what was going to happen after his physical departure from the world: 'It is for your good that I am going away. Unless I go away, the Advocate will not come to you' (John 16:7). One reason for his rejoicing was that presumably he would not be limited in his future ministry as he was during his three years of ministry on earth. The limitation upon him then was that he was restricted to being in one place at one time. If he was in one village and wanted to go to another village, he physically had to leave the place where he was and travel to another area.

The coming of the Holy Spirit changes that. One aspect of the ministry of the Holy Spirit is to enable Jesus to be present in many different places, and in all places. The person of the Holy Spirit is a different person from that of Jesus, but one of the wonders of the Holy Spirit is that he gives himself so that

Jesus is fully present through him. Throughout John chapter 14 Jesus is seeking to share the mystery of his departure and his reappearance at a future time. His new life in his disciples is bound up with the coming of the Holy Spirit.

> *I will ask the Father, and he will give you another advocate to help you and be with you for ever – the Spirit of truth. The world cannot accept him, because it neither sees him nor knows him. But you know him, for he lives in you and will be in you. I will not leave you as orphans; I will come to you.* (John 14:16–18)

Jesus meant that it is not just the Holy Spirit who will be with those disciples, and by extension with everyone who follows Jesus, but Jesus himself. His presence will now be in a way that is not limited by the constraints of geography and time.

So what are we expecting to find as we seek the presence of Jesus? Are we expecting to find his presence in the same way that the disciples experienced him as they journeyed with him in his earthly ministry? No, because the presence of Jesus has changed since then, in that at the end of his time on earth he ascended into heaven from where he reigns. Yet before his crucifixion, Jesus tells his disciples that although he is going away, he will come back to them (John 14:18). This phrase is in the context of the coming of the Holy Spirit. So we can safely assume that any experience of Jesus today is brought to us by the Holy Spirit.

The way that we can experience the presence of Jesus is probably in the realm of the imagination. We often think of the imagination as the part of our mind given to 'making things up'. We speak of people as having lively imaginations, meaning that in some way they are able to escape into a different world and pretend things are real that might not be so. However, imagination is a God-given faculty within us, not simply a release mechanism for coping with the drudgery of life or as a vehicle for creativity. It is a part of us created by him to be a place where he can meet with us. Perhaps it is helpful to think of the imagination as a chamber within us, a place where we can experience the reality of Jesus through means other than our physical senses of sight, sound and touch. In the chamber of our imagination some of us will see Jesus, others will be aware of his presence, some may hear him, and all of us may in some way experience him. One gentleman wrote to tell us what happened to him:

> *I pictured Jesus sitting on the chair behind and beneath me (I was standing up). He asked me to sit on his lap and let him enfold me and ensconce me in safety; this was the safe place to relax I'd always been searching for and had never had. Once I were to relax in to this, I would then be able to walk and move so that my being was freer, lighter and more flexible – and in the process I would be released to do the things he had for me. I don't think I have ever had such a clear and personal message from Jesus in this way before.*

What is happening when we experience the presence of Jesus in this way is that we catch a glimpse of him at a particular time and moment. I believe that the Holy Spirit loves to bring us glimpses of Jesus to be with us there and then. I suspect that if the Spirit brought us *all* the majesty of Jesus and we were standing before the throne of God, it would probably be too much for us. Rather, out of his grace, he gives us these lovely glimpses to increase our fellowship with Jesus on a wonderful on-going basis. There are a number of ways in which we can find a glimpse of the presence of Jesus. We are all different, and you may find one of the ways I'm going to mention more helpful than the others. A question I have come to ask people is: 'Where is Jesus for you right now?' Having asked the question, I encourage people to engage with it and begin to trust that sense of his presence. People tend to sense the presence of Jesus in a number of ways.

Direct encounter

In a direct encounter, people are encouraged to find the presence of Jesus with them. As they are sitting or standing, they are encouraged to focus on where Jesus might be. It may be that they can sense him standing in front of them or by their side. Some might be able to 'see' Jesus; some may not. It is not about visualising him, but rather about tuning in to the reality of him really being there.

> *One man said that as Jesus walked past him he could smell his clothes.*
>
> *I've seen folk reach down and take the hand of Jesus, not necessarily because they could see him, but they just knew he was there.*
>
> *A lady said, 'I just knew he was standing right behind me. I just knew he was there.'*

Of course, Jesus is everywhere, but the people in these instances knew that this was a glimpse of Jesus brought to them at a particular time and place.

We are very careful not to encourage folk to imagine Jesus standing there – it is not something that we want people to initiate by their own power of imagination, but would rather the Holy Spirit bring Jesus to them in the place of their imagination.

One gentleman shared his remarkable encounter with Jesus.

I attended the healing event reluctantly because the one person in the world who really mattered to me had not been healed – my beautiful and beloved wife, who died aged 51. But I had no idea how memorable this day six months later was to be.

I had Jesus right beside me holding me with his left arm firmly around my waist. Then he began to lean his head on mine because he loved me. I pulled my head away, discomforted. 'Isn't it supposed to be the other way round? Aren't I supposed to hold your waist, and lean on you?' I exclaimed. He said nothing, but continued to hold my waist.

Meanwhile, John was saying this was the opportunity to ask Jesus the really big questions – and to expect an answer. I had no questions.

Then John asked us what we were doing with Jesus. I continued to be embarrassed by Jesus still holding me. So I thought we should walk. We walked forward together.

Then Jesus looked at me and said, 'It's OK.' Now I was cross. I raised my voice saying, 'What's OK? How can it be OK? My wife has died; nothing is OK. All the colour and taste has gone out of my life!'

Jesus said nothing. Then he looked down to his right-hand side. I glanced round him to see what he was smiling at. Jesus had his right arm around a woman's waist – and it was my wife who died those six months earlier! I could see her, but she didn't see me. She was looking up into Jesus' face, radiantly happy. He was smiling back at her. There she was, in heaven, in eternity – and here was I, on earth, in time. Yet at this same moment Jesus is walking with us both, together!

Then Jesus looked at me as if to say, 'See?' And I did see. I understood. Wherever Jesus is, it's OK. Jesus didn't use big theological terms; he simply said, 'It's OK.'

For weeks afterward, when I felt sad, or things were unsettled in me, I physically felt that strong arm around my waist. And I learned to lean towards him, grateful for such love.

Finding your secret place

Some people focus on a place that they remember, a place that they naturally think of in their times of prayer. I like to think of these places as secret places where the Lord loves to meet us, and they can be anywhere. It is often not the sacredness of the place that makes it a secret place, but sometimes because people felt the Lord there at some point in the past, and so they naturally return there in their minds to find his presence again.

Someone wrote this to me:

There was a favourite cliff-top walk that I used to enjoy walking along with my family. The views out to sea were spectacular. For a long time, whenever I met with Jesus he would meet me on the bench at the top of those cliffs. Sometimes I would arrive first and he would join me, whereas on other occasions I would approach the seat where I could see him already sitting waiting for me. On one occasion it was so blustery that we swapped round so that he could shelter me from the wind.

This process is not about reliving yesterday's blessings or difficulties, but co-operating with Jesus in going back to a place where he longs to meet us.

Letting Jesus take us to a place he wants us to visit

There are times when Jesus' agenda is quite different from ours. There are probably times or places in our lives we would rather not visit; perhaps there is too much pain associated with those moments. Sometimes Jesus takes people to such places in their moments of encounter with him because there is something that he wants to do there. This is not something that people would usually do of their own initiative, but if that is the place where Jesus spontaneously takes them, then we encourage people to walk with him there.

One lady spoke about how she had felt alone and low, with a sense of being oppressed by a feeling of uselessness. Jesus took her hand and led her to a picture of herself as a little girl on her landing, and then he pointed out that this little girl was lonely. He said, 'I was there – nothing can separate you from the love of God.'

On another occasion, someone shared that when they were asked to find Jesus, they found themselves revisiting the room in which a close family member had died. They had always thought that Jesus had deserted them at that awful time but he clearly showed them that he was in that room with them. Now it's different because they know he was there in that dark place with them – and there was such a sense of joy there.

Encountering Jesus in his Word

Another way that people have found the presence of Jesus is by meditating on the Bible. Many of the gospel stories of Jesus have the hallmarks of being eyewitness accounts of the stories. (Note some of the little details, such as how Bartimaeus throws his cloak aside in Mark 10:50, and the green grass in Mark 6:39.) One of the joys we can have is to enter into the stories as if we were there ourselves. Take time to read a gospel story carefully and slowly a few times until it is utterly familiar. Then close your eyes and put yourself in the story at the beginning. What can you see, what is the landscape like and what sounds can you 'hear'? Where are you in the story – are you in the crowd, or perhaps a bystander or the subject of the story? Can you see Jesus? What is he like as you see him? Then let the story unfold. What happens?

All these encounters with Jesus are as real as we let them be. If we take the conversation seriously, then it is a real conversation between Jesus and us.

At one of our teaching days, a lady shared how she had encountered Jesus. Jesus was sitting down teaching and she sat on the floor at his feet. He touched her hair in a friendly way as he taught. He then said they would go to the crowds outside, but she was afraid and held on to his robe. They walked through the crowds with her holding on, and then sat down and talked together again. She was overcome with the realisation that, 'He doesn't think I'm stupid. He spoke to me face to face. I always thought that I wasn't clever, but this was a real coming together of minds. He accepts me.'

Communicating with Jesus

This brings us to the final part of the encounter between us and Jesus – communication. When we speak to Jesus, we need to say exactly what we want and not what we think we should say or what others tell us. When Jesus called Bartimaeus to him in Mark 10:51, his question to Bartimaeus was simple: 'What do you want me to do for you?' There are probably many things for which Bartimaeus could have asked, but he actually asked for his sight back.

I have seen people ask for many different things when they encounter Jesus. Some people come right out with what is on their heart, just like Bartimaeus did, while others find that when they are face to face with Jesus, what they actually say is different from what they thought they would say.

I remember praying for a young woman who spoke about pain that was bringing great misery to her, yet when she encountered Jesus, tears poured down her cheeks as she expressed her profound love for him. Her initial spoken need took a back seat when she encountered him.

It does not always need to be like this – it certainly wasn't the case for Bartimaeus – and perhaps what Jesus values most is our honesty. There is little point in standing before him imagining that we ought to tell him that we love him, when actually there is something that we are desperate to scream out at him.

There is perhaps another question that needs to be considered, namely why do we have to ask for healing? Why doesn't God simply heal us or do the best for us if he loves us? To this there is no real answer, except to say that Jesus seemed to respond not just to a need, but to people who sought his help. I am often fascinated by the passage in Mark 5 where Jesus gets out of a boat and a large crowd gathers around him. Any crowd has needs, and that crowd was probably no exception. To which need does Jesus respond? To which person does he choose to minister? The answer is that he ministers to the one who asks. In this particular story we read that Jairus comes forward and, kneeling at his feet, pleads with Jesus to come with him. I often wonder what would have

Jesus seemed to respond not just to a need, but to people who sought his help

happened if a person with a different need had pushed ahead of Jairus. We might have quite a different story of healing in place of the one that is there. Similarly in Matthew 8, a large crowd follows Jesus. This time it is a leper who steps up to ask for healing. We are not told what happened to any other lepers or to other sick people who were also in that crowd, but perhaps they didn't receive what the leper received because they did not ask.

This story about the leper says something about us having to be bold enough to bring our needs to him. Asking him about our own needs isn't selfish; it's almost an act of worship. It's like saying, 'Lord, I can't do anything myself. I need you. You're the only one who can help me. So, Lord, here I am.' I believe that Jesus responds to that kind of call. How much clearer could Jesus be when he said to Bartimaeus in Mark 10:51, 'What do you want me to do for you?' Basically he was saying, 'Tell me what you want – just say it,' and the blind man burst out in reply, 'I want to see.'

We often talk about 'intimacy with God', and the impression this phrase gives is of God's intimacy with us. It creates a picture of him being closer to us than would otherwise be the case. However, perhaps intimacy with God begins with our decision to be intimate with him first; with us sharing our hearts and our secrets with him. Perhaps it is only when we begin to be utterly open with God that we can experience his intimacy with us. Intimacy is, of course, a risk, as we have no idea how people will react to us, but with God we know that he is already aware of what is on our hearts. We know he has demonstrated his love to us by sending Jesus and we know he will never reject us. The step towards intimacy is to open our hearts to him.

Communication is not a one-sided business. Prayer is not simply about us talking to God and then walking away. It also involves us listening to what he says. Often people will put themselves in the 'I don't hear God speaking to me' category, and look longingly at those people who seem to be able to hear him speak with crystal-clear clarity. In John 10:1–6, Jesus speaks about us as sheep, and says, 'the sheep listen to his voice' (v3) and 'his sheep know his voice' (v4).

The assumption here seems to be that we can all hear him speaking because he is the shepherd and we are the sheep. If it is true that he speaks and we can hear, perhaps the problem is that we have not learned to recognise his voice. Our expectation may be that God will probably speak with a booming voice, or communicate in blood-red writing on the wall. Actually, his voice is quite natural and easy to miss. It often comes by way of a spontaneous thought that enters our minds, or a picture that suddenly occurs to us, or a verse of Scripture (or Bible reference) that just seems to be there when it wasn't before.

Someone spoke to Jesus, and when they had finished, he said: 'I have heard you.'

Jesus was washing a lady's feet. It was very powerful and she said, 'You can't do this for me.' He replied, 'But I want to. Let me do it.'

A gentleman told Jesus that he wanted to know more of his presence and he said, 'I am with you.'

A lady told Jesus that she was very sorry she had not been close recently, as life had been too busy. Then she had a picture of herself and Jesus walking towards each other. Jesus held out his hands and said how much he loved her and gave her a cuddle. He was so gentle, warm and tender.

'Jesus had his arm round my shoulder, and I felt a deep and rich sense of peace.'

We do have a habit of analysing (and doubting) what we feel God is saying to us and some people have developed the practice of talking to God with a paper and pen in their hands. As they feel God is speaking to them, they write down what he says without thinking about it too much. It is good practice to write down what God says; we can always test and filter it later, but it is much harder to test what we have already forgotten.

This brings us to the question of how do we test what God is saying to us? Most of us are naturally cautious, and don't want to be misled or led astray or simply follow what might be the meaningless product of a hyped-up imagination. Perhaps one of the biggest problems we face when we are dealing with God speaking to us is our faith. We simply do not believe what he is saying to us. Our natural expectation is for God to speak correction to us and we actually find it very hard to receive his unconditional love. **Most people probably have more faith in their ability to be misled than in the ability of God to talk to us**, so we probably disregard much of what God is saying. Having said that, what steps can we take to increase the sense of peace that what we are hearing is actually the voice of God?

It helps to recognise that there are probably other voices within us, all clamouring for attention. The first is the voice of our preconceptions. We all carry preconceived ideas from a number of sources, either things we have been told or things we have taken on board from experiences in life. Such preconceived ideas might not be very helpful, but they still have a voice. This voice may well be saying that we are worthless; any number of people may have told us this, and it can be a small logical step to assume that God feels the same way. When we come into an encounter with Jesus, it takes a moment to disengage from what we assume he may say, and which we assume is probably something derogatory or even nothing at all. This is why we encourage people to pay attention to the spontaneous thoughts that come into their minds in these times of 'encounter', because it is these spontaneous thoughts that are often the opposite of our preconceived ideas of what we think God will say.

The other voice that is often present – and even Jesus had to battle with this voice – is the voice of the devil, the one who loves to seek to rob us of the unconditional love that God wants to pour into our hearts.

Paul gives us a general rule about identifying the voice of God in his first letter to the Corinthians. He describes the phenomena of prophecy, whereby someone senses they have something that God wants to speak to another person. Paul's principle is that such words are for 'strengthening, encouraging and comfort' (1 Corinthians 14:3). It is fair to assume that the words that God speaks to us out of love fall into that category. (There may indeed be times when God wants to correct us, but rather than doing it in a way that brings condemnation, his correction comes in ways that are also encouraging to us.)

There is also the issue of consistency – the God who meets with us and speaks with us is also the one who inspired the words of the Bible. The words he speaks to us will be entirely consistent with the truths to which the Bible testifies.

A woman shared her story of meeting Jesus. She told him how mundane her life was. Then she saw him as her playmate in her lounge at home, building towers, giggling, washing up, and so on. She had a real sense of contentment that that was the place to be with him; that it was OK not to be busy blessing people as she used to. The words spoken over Jesus came to mind: 'This is my Son with whom I am well pleased.' She asked, 'Why would you be well pleased with me?' He immediately gave her a huge long list of things, ending with 'Because it is a pleasure to be around you. Just because I am!'

When we have a sense of God speaking to us, a good practice is to ask, 'Why is God saying this to me? Is God saying that he loves me precisely because this is something that I find difficult to believe or accept easily?' If that is so, then we have a response to make, namely to take God's words, find the biblical truths that underline them, accept them and allow them to sink deeper and deeper into our being.

Sometimes God's communication with us is an active touch of healing. The following are beautiful accounts of Jesus touching people in need. In both of these stories no one prayed for these ladies and no one laid hands on them – and yet they were touched wonderfully by Jesus.

This first story is written by a lady who came to a seminar we were leading at an exhibition:

You invited me to share my experience at the Christian Resources Exhibition and it is a pleasure to do so. For years I have suffered with pain in my feet due to severely collapsed bone structures and resultant arthritis and tendon pain. I found your facilitation of healing prayer at the end of your seminar to be very powerful. When you asked us, 'Where is Jesus for you at this moment?' I had a visual image of him before me. And when you subsequently asked, 'What do you want to ask Jesus to heal?' I just said, 'My feet: please bring healing to my feet.' Immediately I felt something happening. The only way I can describe it is that it felt as if things were moving around vigorously inside my feet. My feet felt 'alive with inner activity'. At the end of the session these sensations remained strong and I simply took myself to a quiet area to just sit with the Lord and allow whatever was happening to happen. It was an amazing sensation and took about half an hour to subside.

After that I was able to walk round the exhibition for several hours and my feet were entirely comfortable and had no pain. In fact, it felt as if I was dancing on air. I would not normally have been able to do this for more than an hour without developing quite a painful limp!

Though not fully healed, my feet changed shape to the point where my podiatrist prescribed orthotics of a different shape, and since that time I have never been in pain with my feet! What a wonderful God we have!

On another occasion when people were being encouraged to speak their needs to Jesus, another lady brought to him a very different kind of need than in the story above. She also testifies to the healing touch of Jesus:

I have been caring for my father for a few years and he has recently gone into a home, where he is very happy. I have had an extremely difficult and traumatic life, particularly in my childhood and in my relationship with my father. My father miraculously came to the Lord and our relationship has been reconciled in an incredible way. However, I have deep sadness and grief since he went to the home a few weeks ago. I have been traumatised and felt a very painful loneliness. On Sunday, I asked Jesus if he would come into those traumatised and lonely places, particularly into my childhood. I felt his hands on my shoulders, and the love and warmth that came through to me was incredible. I asked Jesus why I was so alone, and could he heal my broken heart. Jesus said, 'I was there with you, and I am with you now.'

As an exercise in personal prayer, the 'encounter' is something we can practise by ourselves on a regular basis. The more we do it, the more the creativity of God shines through as we discover him meeting with us and speaking in new and fresh ways.

Father
Son
Spirit

The third focus is on the Holy Spirit. It is not that we are suddenly turning our attention to him because he has been kept waiting, trying to get a look in! Actually the Spirit has been deeply active throughout this time of opening ourselves to God.

We have already noted that he has been at work within us, calling out 'Abba, Father'. Whenever we encounter Jesus in some way, it is the Holy Spirit who brings him to us. However, at this stage it is the power of the Holy Spirit that we are seeking because it is through him that the transforming touch of Jesus comes to us today.

The Holy Spirit is, of course, always with us. Paul points out that our physical bodies are temples of his presence (1 Corinthians 6:19), but there is even more to it than this. The invitation is to open ourselves to him and allow him to bring the transforming touch of Jesus to us.

There is a moment in John's Gospel when Jesus stood up at the Festival of Tabernacles and said: 'If anyone is thirsty, let him come to me and drink. Whoever believes in me, as the Scripture has said, streams of living water will flow from within him' (John 7:37–38, NIV 1984).

It is interesting to give some thought to the final word. Who is the 'him' from whom streams of living water will flow? Some understand this to refer to the believer, that as we align ourselves with Jesus through faith the Spirit flows like living water from us. Yet others suggest that 'him' refers to Jesus, believing that as we connect with him the door is opened for the Spirit to flow from him. It could be both, but it is certainly a challenging thought that as people find the presence of Jesus there is a natural flow of the Holy Spirit simply because Jesus is present.

As we bear in mind this natural flowing of the Spirit, let's seek more of him. This might be as simple as inviting him to increase his presence with us and having the confidence that he will come.

A little later in this book we will look at the effects of the power of the Holy Spirit, but at this stage it is sufficient to note that he is the one who so often brings to us many of the things for which we long.

Consider these verses:

God's love has been poured out into our hearts through the Holy Spirit. (Romans 5:5)

May the God of hope fill you with all joy and peace as you trust in him, so that you may overflow with hope by the power of the Holy Spirit. (Romans 15:13)

By the power of signs and wonders, through the power of the Spirit of God. (Romans 15:19)

Guard the good deposit that was entrusted to you – guard it with the help of the Holy Spirit who lives in us.
(2 Timothy 1:14)

These verses indicate something of the breadth of the activity of the Holy Spirit. If we are in need of more knowledge of God's love, an increase of hope, the power of his healing touch or the strengthening of any of these things, then it is the Holy Spirit who will bring them to us.

9
TRYING IT FOR OURSELVES

You may feel at this point that you would like to try this encounter for yourself. This section is designed to help you do just that. Take it as slowly as you like, and don't feel constrained by the individual parts of this prayer.

In preparation for this encounter, find somewhere quiet where you won't be disturbed and have a notepad and pen to hand.

Before you begin a time of encounter, it might be worth taking a few deep breaths and consciously handing over to God anything that might be at the forefront of your mind so that you can let him do whatever he wants to do in this time.

Begin by taking a few minutes to let the words '*Abba, Father*' run through your mind. Seek to catch the intimacy of a young child approaching the Father they love and trust. You might find it helpful to remind yourself that you were chosen before the foundation of the world, and that he chose to adopt you so that he could pour out his love upon you.

If past experience of the lack of a father's love is something that gets in the way, then find in the person of Jesus a reflection of who the Father is. It might be necessary to break off and perhaps read one of the gospel stories about Jesus. Let the story reveal something to you of the nature of God the Father.

Try and stay at this stage until you have a sense of security in the love of God. This is not being self-indulgent, rather it is being obedient to the command of Jesus to remain in his love (John 15:9).

When you are comfortable in this place, turn to the *presence of Jesus*.

Ask the Holy Spirit to bring you a glimpse of the person of Jesus, and then ask yourself where he is for you at this precise moment. The way we answer that question may well depend upon our personality, so there certainly is no right or wrong answer to this question; but as you sit there, where would you say he is? The sense that comes to you may even seem ridiculous or far-fetched, but stay with it and relax. It might seem a very distant or vague awareness but again, stay with it however vague it may be. Ask yourself how it feels to be in his presence? It is not just about letting Jesus be with you, it is also about giving yourself permission to be there.

> *Some time ago, I wrote about encountering Jesus in our CHM newsletter, and I encouraged people to try to find him or be aware of him wherever they were at that time. A lady wrote back saying, 'I sensed the Lord was standing behind me with his right hand on my right shoulder, and then he leaned down and kissed the top of my head and started stroking my hair.'*

Once again, savour the time you spend in his presence. There is no need to rush to fill the moment with words. Simply be there.

When it feels right, speak to Jesus. What is it you want to say to him? Don't feel bound by what you feel you ought to say to him – say whatever is on your heart. Some people find it helpful to write down what they are saying. What this does is to create an expectation that he is going to speak to you.

Let Jesus speak back to you. Hearing his voice is a matter of being aware of the spontaneous thoughts that come to you. What has come to your mind that was not there before? The 'voice' of Jesus may take the form of a seemingly random thought, or a verse from the Bible. However it comes, write it down and give yourself time to ponder what he is saying. Develop this into a conversation, speaking out or writing your questions and thoughts to God, and recording what he is saying.

It is good to pay attention to other things that might also be happening, perhaps even physical touches of his presence.

This is your encounter with Jesus. When you have finished, take a moment to reflect on it.

- What is the overall thing you have come away with from this time?

- How has it left you feeling?

- What difference does it make to you?

Having met with Jesus in a 'formal' setting at a healing service at the Christian Healing Mission, I was not really prepared for what happened in my living room in my own home a few days later. Although I have learned since becoming a Christian some 18 years ago that Jesus is more than capable of showing up in many varied and different settings and circumstances, I have, too often, been a little shy of asking too much of him outside church or more 'formal' settings. However, one evening at home, while reading a good Christian book which stirred things inside me, I decided to pray. At the time I was suffering from the latest bout of severe back pain and sciatica. At the Healing Mission I had received some wonderful gifts of healing during a healing service. Still experiencing a real degree of related discomfort in my hip region, I decided to pray about it some more. Down went the book and I began to pray using the model we were encouraged to use at the Healing Mission. I went to meet with Jesus and found him waiting for me. All I can say is that, over the next 30 minutes or so, I had a very similar encounter with Jesus to that which I had experienced at the Healing Mission. But this time it was happening in my own home! And without the help/direction/guidance of an ordained minister or trained prayer minister! How amazing is that?! I was excited to accept the healing Jesus was offering me and found a real difference in the flexibility and pain in that misbehaving hip.

I would really love to encourage others to seek to encounter Jesus ANYWHERE. He is so loving and gracious that I would venture to suggest that he will NEVER fail to show up and give you some of his unbounding love.

Again, without any sense of rushing, turn your attention to the person of the *Holy Spirit*. He dwells within you – your body is his temple – so what you are asking for is not so much that he will come to you but that you will experience a deeper overflowing of his presence within you.

A good place to begin is to thank him for his presence and ask for more, in this way surrendering yourself to more of his leading and his power. It may be that there are specific needs that you want to bring to him. Wait patiently and see what you sense is happening.

PART

3

LETTING JESUS
HEAL THROUGH US

10
RECALLING WHO WE ARE

At the beginning of this book there was some time given to pondering the question of who we really are and looking at some of the beautiful truths about this in the Bible. Far from being 'ordinary people', we are temples of God's Holy Spirit and people who bear his name and his presence.

However, the aim of our Christian lives is not just that we can find blessing for ourselves, but that we might also be carriers of God to those around us. Living for Jesus means that we live in the presence of the transforming God, but it also means that we live in the presence of the one who is committed to changing the world. If we wait until we are perfect before we take his presence to others, we will never make a start. Jesus sent out his disciples without him well before they

> ... we live in the presence of the one who is committed to changing the world

were fully functioning reflections of him (Luke 9:1–6). From the very moment we realise who we are we become missionaries, carrying this truth to those whose paths we cross.

There are two ways in which we are called to lift our eyes solely from looking at ourselves to looking at those around us. The first stems from the reality of who we are. We have already looked at four words that Paul uses to describe us: chosen, adopted, forgiven and marked. These are all words that have real significance for us as individuals, but they are also words that have a bearing in our relationship to others. We were chosen before the foundation of the world to live amongst others, sharing our lives with them. We were adopted, along with countless others, to be a part of the family of God, living not in isolation from those around us but sharing with them as brothers and sisters in Christ. We were forgiven, not just that our personal sins might be forgiven but also that we might share that forgiveness with others, 'forgiving each other, just as in Christ God forgave you' (Ephesians 4:32). Interestingly, the very next verse goes on to encourage us to 'Follow God's example . . . live a life of love' (Ephesians 5:1–2). Our imitating of God cannot be done behind individual closed doors, but in our relationships with other people. The fourth word that Paul used was 'marked'. At the end of Luke's Gospel, Jesus gives his disciples his last instructions before he ascends to heaven and sends the Holy Spirit to them. He very much links the fact that they are witnesses to the giving of the Holy Spirit, who will be for them the power of God (Luke 24:48–49). The giving of the Spirit is not an experience to enjoy simply for ourselves, but rather it is something that is the power for us to bless other people in whatever way God calls us. There is then a calling upon all of us to go out, to reach out to others, to help them in ways that are probably well beyond our natural abilities and talents. It is the very fact that we may feel that we have not got within ourselves what others need that is the reason that we have been marked with the presence of the Holy Spirit – it is not just for ourselves, but for others.

The second way in which we are called to be a help to others is that we can pass on to others what we have discovered about God for ourselves. In this, every one of us is a living resource to those around us. In 2 Corinthians 1:4, Paul talks about the God 'who comforts us in all our troubles, so that we can comfort those in any trouble with the comfort we ourselves receive from God.' What Paul is saying is that the things we receive from God are like a deposit in our lives that we can use to help other people.

Presumably the reason that we are able to help others is because if we have experienced his help in some area of our lives, whatever it might be, then we know God is able to bring help to others in those circumstances. Of course, it is also true that there is the danger that because God has blessed us in a particular way, we assume everyone else is going to be similarly blessed whether or not they need or want it!

One of the particular aspects of God's character that we looked at in Part 1 was that of God the provider. It is therefore worth reviewing what the truth of this is for us. How have we experienced the provision of God in our lives? Our initial thought may be that he has not provided for us in any real or tangible way, but consider this list of possible ways in which we may have received God's provision and see if any of them resonates:

- financial provision

- the provision of healing

- the giving of strength and patience

- the provision of people to come alongside us at the right time

- the giving of an opportunity to bring help to another

- victory over a particular temptation or sin

- the giving of gifts by which we can be of service.

The list could go on, but it is worth noting the particular comforts that God has given you so that you can, with confidence, pass on the comfort of God the provider to other people. This does not mean that unless you have experienced something similar to someone else you cannot minister to them, but certainly if we can find our own story of God's provision to us, we will more readily 'own' the truth of God the provider which we can readily share with others.

Another aspect of this name 'provider' that we carry as his name-bearers is this: Abraham was called to do something very dramatic in sacrificing his son, but God provided the means for him to carry out the sacrifice by providing a ram instead. We are called to be bearers of the presence of God to others, but we may feel unworthy or ill-equipped to do the task he is calling us to. We may feel we do not have the right words to say, nor the power within us to bring about the change a person needs from God. We may even feel that we lack the patience needed to bring the things of God to others.

. . . it is precisely because we do not have the means in our own strength that we need what God can give us

At those moments, we need to remember that it is God who is the provider and it is not something we are meant to provide from our own strength or wisdom. God provided Abraham with what he needed, and he will provide whatever we feel we are lacking as we aim to carry out his will. The point of God being the provider was precisely because Abraham could not meet his own need – because of what Abraham did not have, he needed God to be the provider. Similarly with us, it is precisely because we do not have the means in our own strength that we need what God can give us.

11
IS HEALING A GIFT?

A question that might arise is not so much one of provision, but one of gifting. The Bible speaks of some people being specially gifted for ministry – what if we do not feel that we have such a gifting? It is certainly true that Paul speaks about those who are specifically gifted in various ministries and healing is one such gift (1 Corinthians 12:9). It is likely that what Paul envisaged was that there would be those within the church who are recognised as having specific gifts such as healing. There is probably something about their character that makes them approachable, and there is something about their faith that allows them to see beyond the present situations that might be afflicting people and to hold onto the promises that God has for this person. There is something about their persistence that allows them to keep hold of the vision for healing, even when others are ready to give up. There is also something inexplicable about them, that when they pray for the sick things seem to happen more than when other people say the same words. Such people have a gift of healing. This is similar to the way that some people have a particular gift for teaching. We all know people whose teaching can lift us up and reveal the wonders of God in a way that moves us, and then there are those who often leave

> . . . a gift of healing grows and develops over a period of time

us more confused than when they started. However, it is likely that a gift of healing grows and develops over a period of time – involving many disappointments, many questions and probably quite a few mistakes along the way. This is true of all the gifts. It is interesting that in 1 Corinthians 14:12 Paul encourages his readers to 'try to excel' in gifts, which implies practice, trial and perseverance. So perhaps rather than asking, 'How do I know if I have this particular gift?' a better question would be, 'How do I know that I haven't?'

The fact that there are some people who may have evident gifts certainly doesn't mean that anyone should be dissuaded from praying for others according to their need. If we have a sense that we could pray for someone's healing, it is not right to compare ourselves to other people and wish that someone else were there instead. At that moment, we are the presence of the healing Jesus to that person and it is time to be what we are called to be. The very fact that healing is something that interests you and draws you to find out more may well be an indication that this is a growing gift within you, something that God is planting. It is therefore certainly right that you seek opportunities to practise, pray and learn about what God may be planting in your heart. Jesus does not seem to advocate that we should not pray for healing because we are not sure that we are gifted to do so. In John 15:5, Jesus says, 'If you remain in me and I in you, you will bear much fruit.' In the context of a healing ministry, 'fruit' refers to the effectiveness of our ministry. What Jesus is saying is that what is more important than anything is our relationship with him. The approach to praying for healing that I have been advocating in this book is not one that relies on human knowledge or understanding, or even whether we are gifted or not, but rather one that relies heavily upon the person for whom we are praying having an encounter with Jesus and finding what flows from that.

> . . . seek opportunities to practise, pray and learn about what God may be planting in your heart

12
WHAT MAKES A GOOD PRAYER MINISTER?

Christian healing is a divine activity: unless God touches somebody when they come for prayer, nothing is likely to happen. They may feel loved or comforted, but it is the touch of God that is actually going to bring change to them.

Having said this, generally speaking God uses people like us in this ministry, so the way we interact with those who ask for prayer is very important. We can be wonderful 'doorways' for people to meet with God, but also quite effective barriers. Of course, God can work through anyone – but this is not a licence for us to make it as difficult as we can for him! So how should we interact with people and what are some of the values we should adopt in order to make it easier for people to meet with Jesus?

1. Our role is to help people encounter God

Our role as prayer ministers is to help people encounter the living God. This involves assuring them of the Father's deep love for them, reminding them of the presence of Jesus and welcoming the power of the Holy Spirit. There may be any number of factors why this may not always happen just as we might like, but if we don't make this our aim then there is far less chance of an encounter with God happening at all.

The aim of our ministry is not to display our skills, wisdom and gifts, but to do all we can to facilitate a person's meeting with the living God. It can be so releasing not having to come up with the right things to say, nor bearing the responsibility for making the correct diagnosis about a person's situation.

2. Our role is to treat people with respect and dignity

Throughout Matthew's Gospel there are moments when the author pauses to reflect on some aspect of the ministry of Jesus. He often did this by referring to a quotation from the Old Testament, such as Matthew 12:18–21. Matthew had just recorded some wonderful accounts of Jesus healing the sick and in verse 20 he reflected on the ministry of Jesus with a quote from Isaiah: 'A bruised reed he will not break, and a smouldering wick he will not snuff out.'

This describes how Jesus treated people; he was gentle and he didn't break them. So it follows that if this was how Jesus responded to people, we should aim to do likewise. Basically this comes down to treating people as we would like to be treated ourselves.

So what does this mean in practice? Suppose you had a deep dark secret that you knew you needed to share with somebody. It is unlikely that you would go up to the first person you met in the coffee queue and tell them about it! Instead you would probably be selective and look for a person with particular gifts and the sort of character that you felt you could approach, perhaps someone with discretion, gentleness and empathy who would listen carefully to you without judging or checking their emails or watch every two minutes. As well as this, it would be important to find someone who exhibited a firm faith and the expectation that God would bring his transforming touch to the situation.

The challenge is that if this describes the qualities that we would look for in a prayer minister, then it is likely that they are also what people want to see in us.

3. Our role is to minister and not pass judgement

Jesus seemed to have an amazing ability to pray for those in need without letting anything else get in the way. He appeared to make very few demands on people before ministering to them, and was quite unfazed if their theology was not perfect. There is a story in John 9 of Jesus healing a man who had been born blind. When the authorities questioned the man about Jesus after he had been healed, he simply said in verse 25: 'Whether he is a sinner or not, I don't know. One thing I do know. I was blind but now I see!' This man did not know much about Jesus and his theology was certainly not well developed, but that didn't stop Jesus reaching out and doing something miraculous in his life.

> **Jesus seemed to have an amazing ability to pray for those in need without letting anything else get in the way**

Jesus seemed to value faith but he didn't appear to ask too many questions about it. After all, he raised Lazarus from the dead and Lazarus was certainly not exhibiting much faith at the time! Jesus was delighted when faith was present, but this didn't seem to be the deciding factor about whether or not the person was healed. Nor did Jesus seem to demand repentance before he ministered to people. There is even the story about the man they called Legion since he had so many unclean spirits within him, but there was no discussion about how the spirits got there and no urge for him to repent before Jesus brought about change.

One of my favourite stories about transformation is not even listed as a healing story, despite recounting a massive change in someone's life. It is the story of Zacchaeus, who was so fascinated by Jesus that he climbed a tree in order to see him, only to learn that Jesus planned to stay at his house that day. Tax collectors, like Zacchaeus, tended to be unpopular because they often collected more money than their entitlement, but when Jesus spoke to him there was no judgement or condemnation, no mention of his sin, and yet something about being acknowledged and cared for by Jesus seems to have been enough to touch his heart and cause him to make restitution to those whom he had wronged.

4. Our role is to listen and not to make assumptions

We can all be prone to making assumptions about those coming to us for prayer. It is easy for us to assume that we know what they want and sometimes, even as we see them approaching, we can begin to guess what their needs might be. Many years ago, I had the great privilege of leading a healing service for a group of deaf people. Just before the service, the chaplain spoke to me and asked me not to assume that the main issue for these people was their lack of hearing – and she was absolutely right. Deafness was never mentioned as I went around asking people for their prayer requests, but it would have been so easy to assume that this would be a major concern for them all.

It is also easy to assume that the way in which we prayed for the last person will be suitable when we pray for the next person. However, it is important to remember that everyone is different, with their own individual stories, histories and needs. We are all God's unique children, and part of the respect and dignity that we want to give to people is to remember this and treat them as such.

5. Our role is to offer ministry in a way that is accessible to people of every tradition

Not everyone that we pray for is like us! They may not speak like us, practise their faith as we do, interpret Scripture in the same way as us or even live a lifestyle that we consider to be normal or acceptable. Our role as a prayer minister is not to expect them to be like us nor to conform to our standards.

Not everyone that we pray for is like us!

We also need to take care with the language that we use. It can be so easy for Christians to lapse into jargon with phrases such as 'the lamb of God' or 'leaving burdens at the cross'. These may be clear and powerful images for us, but others may not understand what we mean by them, and we need to make sure that the phrases and statements we make can be easily understood.

It is also good to watch out for any practices we have that seem perfectly natural to us but may be distracting for others. One example of this is praying in tongues. If the person receiving prayer has never experienced this before, or does not believe that it is a valid practice, it is likely to distract them and they may even feel unable to enter into the ministry – especially if the tongues are spoken aloud out of the blue with no warning. If praying in tongues is an important practice for you, I would encourage you to do it quietly so that the person for whom you are praying isn't even aware of it.

The 'laying on of hands' is another example of what might seem a perfectly natural action on our part, but is one that can cause offence or be hard for some people. I remember praying for a group of young people years ago, and as I was praying I simply put a hand on each one of them. Afterwards they shared what the Lord had been doing, and one man said that he had been totally put off because I had touched him and he did not like being touched. He was quite right – I had no right to touch him without permission and there may have been any number of reasons why this was hard for him. It is always good practice to ask permission before laying a hand on someone else.

It should be said at this point that the laying on of hands is just that – a hand being laid upon someone. It does not involve stroking, massaging, shaking or anything else! Such actions can be so distracting to the person receiving prayer.

6. Our role is to bring faith and expectation to a situation

It is important to treat the people who turn to us for prayer with respect and care, but we are called to offer more than this. Our role is to have faith. It can be very revealing to pause before starting to pray and consider what we actually expect to happen. We will be looking at ways of increasing our faith a little further on in this book, but it is largely about looking at the person of Jesus and catching his heart for those who are sick.

It may be something of a generalisation, but the two most likely reasons for lack of faith on our part are because we are simply overwhelmed by the problem, or because we have not seen Jesus act in response to our prayers in the past. Let's look at each of these briefly.

What are we looking at?

We have already discussed beginning prayer with a focus on the Father rather than on the problem facing us and this is probably one of the greatest things we can do when we are praying for someone else. The person for whom we are praying may well be absorbed in their situation, and to help lift their vision from their problem so that they can re-focus on the nature of God is so important.

Have we seen God work in answer to our prayers in the past?

Judging God's ability to work through us by what we have seen him do in the past can be so discouraging, as the truth is that often we have little idea of how he answers our prayers since we can only judge the results by what happens there and then in front of our eyes. Suppose for some reason there is a time delay between our prayers and the response, or if someone doesn't tell us how God used us in prayer ministry? We might well be discouraged because nothing seems to happen as a result of our prayers, whereas the reality may well be very different.

Above are some of the values that I believe we should try to exhibit when we are involved in prayer ministry. It is not meant to be an exhaustive list of dos and don'ts, but simply pointers to enable us to be the very best we possibly can be at this ministry.

13
BEGINNING BY LISTENING

The occasions when we pray for others may be varied. It may conclude a conversation over coffee at home or it may take place in church. Our ministry may be to lift that person up in intercession before God. However we see our ministry, there are perhaps two important steps to take and both involve listening.

The first step is to listen to the truth and not to our feelings. It is natural to feel quite overcome with either panic or a sense of helplessness before starting to pray. Everything we thought we would remember goes out of our heads and we suddenly haven't got a clue what to do. At this point we have to come right back to the truth of who we are: we are a temple of the Holy Spirit and we bear the name of the Lord God Almighty. It is not our words or our wisdom that are going to make any difference to this situation, but rather the activity of God working through us. It is always worth pausing to call to mind who we are as we begin to pray for someone. The temptation is to rush straight into prayer as a matter of urgency. It is always a good thing to pause to give ourselves time to reflect on who we are and what it is that we are doing.

The first step is to listen to the truth and not to our feelings

The next stage is to listen to the person we are about to pray for. Is listening actually that important? In all the gospel stories about the healing ministry of Jesus, it is interesting that we do not have much record of Jesus spending any length of time listening to people's stories. In fact, he seems quite uninterested about why people had the particular issues that caused them suffering. Even those who were suffering from oppression and possession by evil spirits were not quizzed as to possible causes for their affliction. Why is listening so important, especially as our aim is to bring people into a direct encounter with the person of Jesus? Why do *we* need to hear their story?

There are perhaps two main reasons why it is important to listen. The first is that listening reflects Christ's ministry of connecting with the world. The salvation that Jesus brought was not to look down from heaven and dispense help as if from a divine slot machine. Rather, he entered into our world and lived among us. By doing so, he made that deep connection with our need. That is the love that he showed, and is therefore the type of love that we are to emulate. Our calling as ministers, in whatever capacity we are called to minister, is to make connections to those in need and minister from those connections. For all of us, a simple connection that we can all make is to be available to listen to people. By being willing to listen, we are entering into people's lives and experiences in a way that is similar to how Jesus enters into our lives and experiences.

The second reason for listening is that as someone shares their story, they are allowing a door to be opened to bring the light of Jesus into that situation. If someone is keen to keep their story private, there is the likelihood that they do not see how that situation can be remedied or helped, but when their story is shared with another the door is opened for a new perspective, another interpretation about what God can do in that situation. By listening to their story, we are allowing new light to be shed in the darkness – and by simply being there and bearing his name, we are creating an opportunity for Jesus to connect with them and their story.

Listening is not always easy and many things can get in the way. It may be something within us – our own unease with what is being shared, even our boredom if we are not particularly interested. It may be a matter of being distracted, either by background noise or by something else that is on our mind. There are probably techniques that we can learn to listen better, but it probably begins with the humbling realisation that this person matters so much to God that Jesus came to die for them. He is not bored, nor distracted; they have his full attention. In fact, it is interesting to note that on some occasions Jesus was so attentive to the person to whom he was ministering that he took steps to change the environment in which the ministry was taking place.

. . . this person matters so much to God that Jesus came to die for them

In Mark chapter 7, for example, some people approached Jesus to ask him to heal a man who was deaf and could not speak. In verse 33, we read, 'He took him aside, away from the crowd.' Similarly, in the following chapter, people brought a blind man to Jesus for healing: 'He took the blind man by the hand and led him outside the village' (Mark 8:23). We may also want to change the physical environment around us if there is a lot of background noise; would a quiet room be better? Would it also be better to find an occasion when there is more time available?

Jesus did not just seek to change the physical environment, he also broke into the environment of attitude. He often did this with the questions he asked. Some of his questions may seem strange to us, but actually what he seemed to be doing was using direct questions to break into people's thought patterns. He asked two blind men, 'Do you believe that I am able to do this?' (Matthew 9:28). On another occasion, he put a very blunt question to a man who had been crippled for 38 years: 'Do you want to get well?' (John 5:6). Of course we want to be as gentle and sensitive as we can, but there are times when it is very helpful to seek to break into what can be a very negative environment, such as the continual re-telling of the story or repeating the wrongs that have been done. A gentle and effective way of doing this is to ask the question inspired by what Jesus asked of Bartimaeus: 'What is it you want God to do for you?' Sometimes people can be so caught up in their stories that they have not really considered what they actually want God to do. Once people begin to engage with that question, then the possibilities of what God can do begin to open up.

14
THE THREE ASPECTS OF HEALING PRAYER

We often think of Jesus' healing ministry as being quite varied, sometimes involving touch, at other times a command, or even both. Actually, as we look a little closer at the stories, what we notice is that in the majority of them we can discover three elements that seem to occur in most of the stories. First, they involve an *encounter* with Jesus. Second, the presence of *faith* is evident, either in the person seeking prayer, in someone connected with them or even perhaps in the person of Jesus himself. The third element is that of *power*, which seems to be transferred either by touch or by a word, or both. Let us look at a few examples.

In Matthew 8:1–3 we read of the leper who was healed by Jesus:

> *When Jesus came down from the mountainside, large crowds followed him. A man with leprosy came and knelt before him and said, 'Lord, if you are willing, you can make me clean.' Jesus reached out his hand and touched the man. 'I am willing,' he said. 'Be clean!' Immediately he was cleansed of his leprosy.*

We can see these three elements of encounter, faith and power within this story. This encounter was initiated by the leper, who recognised there was something special about Jesus. Jesus didn't seem to go out of his way to minister to the leper; rather it was the leper who chose to come to Jesus. As regards faith, there was an element of faith already present within the leper, which is why he approached Jesus. That fledgling faith must have soared when

Jesus declared his intention to bring healing. Power then flowed when Jesus reached out to touch the man and spoke cleansing to the man's body.

We can see the same three elements in another story from Matthew's Gospel – the story of the healing of two blind men in Matthew 9:27–31:

As Jesus went on from there, two blind men followed him, calling out, 'Have mercy on us, Son of David!' When he had gone indoors, the blind men came to him, and he asked them, 'Do you believe that I am able to do this?' 'Yes, Lord,' they replied. Then he touched their eyes and said, 'According to your faith let it be done to you'; and their sight was restored. Jesus warned them sternly, 'See that no one knows about this.' But they went out and spread the news about him all over that region.

This encounter occurred when the blind men came to Jesus seeking healing. They expressed their faith by approaching him in the first place, but Jesus seemed to want more from them. By asking them explicitly whether they believed that he could do what they asked, he drew them to a new level of faith and it was their response to his question that revealed the depth of it. The power that released healing came when Jesus touched their eyes and spoke healing to them.

If these three elements seemed to be so important in the way that Jesus dealt with those who came to him, perhaps these are the elements that we should be seeking to foster as we develop our relationship with him and seek his transformation. These different elements may seem like a lot to remember, or it may seem as if we are building a structure that appears too rigid to allow for any movement or freedom. Perhaps a better way of thinking about this healing process is that of train lines. Rather than constricting drivers, the tracks actually liberate them and free them from having to plot a course between A and B. There are still decisions to be made (perhaps not by the driver) about the speed of the train at certain points along the way, and where the stops should be made and for how long, but the course itself is decided. These three elements are evident in the ministry of Jesus, so perhaps the course has been plotted for us. We do have some decisions to make as to when we pause and which parts to emphasise, but we know where we are heading.

1. Encounter

What I have been sharing in this book is that one of the aims of prayer ministry is to bring people to a position where they can encounter the living Jesus, to speak to him for themselves and hear his voice in their lives. I have suggested that a simple way of doing this is to think of three spotlights being turned on in turn – the light of the Father's love, the light of the presence of Jesus and the light of the power of the Spirit. We have already explored how we might use this to find God for ourselves, but now let's turn to look at bringing other people into this consciousness.

Father

The difficulty here is that we do not know what someone's experience of the word 'father' is. If we start straight away by telling them how wonderful Father God is, when their experience of the word 'father' is negative, it is likely that they will become detached from this time of prayer. Explanation is never a wasted process, so it might be helpful to begin by explaining that we are going to spend a few moments in the worship of Father; that he is the Father of the Lord Jesus Christ as well as our Father. This may not change their views of fatherhood, but at least they will know what we are doing.

It is also worth remembering that we are involved in a spiritual activity, and if it is true that the Spirit of God is at work in them calling out 'Abba, Father', then the words we are speaking are being echoed within that person by the Spirit of God. It is not simply down to us to phrase the prayer in such a wonderful way that the person will grasp it, but we are at work with the Spirit of God and it is his ministry that will make the difference.

When praying for people, I encourage them to try to say 'yes' inwardly as I am praying, rather than countering every prayer with an inner 'but'. Co-operation is about opening doors, and their saying 'yes' is a wonderful way for them to open the door to what God is seeking to do.

It is up to us to gently lead a time of verbal worship to the Father, seeking to make it as genuine as we can, so that it connects with what the Holy Spirit is doing within us and within them, as he calls out those words 'Abba, Father'. There are no set words that need to be used in a repetitive manner, but it can be helpful to ponder in worship some of the following truths:

● He is the 'Father of our Lord Jesus Christ', and '[our] Father' (Ephesians 1:3, John 20:17).

● He 'chose [this person] . . . before the creation of the world' (Ephesians 1:4).

- He has adopted them so that the love he has for Jesus might be the same love he pours upon them (Ephesians 1:5, John 17:26).

- 'His love endures forever' (Psalm 136:1).

Our words do not have to be extensive. It is likely that, as we pray, the person receiving prayer is going to be processing what we are saying and letting it sink in, as well as hopefully making our prayers personal for them. For this reason, times of silence are just as important as the words we speak. It is in the silence that the truth can really sink in. A great mistake in ministry is to feel that we have to fill in all the gaps with words. We do not, and indeed too many words can be a real distraction.

Son

Perhaps one of the most common mistakes we can make as we seek to bring people into the presence of Jesus is to give the impression that they have to 'see' or 'visualise' Jesus. It may well be that Jesus comes to them in a visual way, but he may not. I remember praying with a man who knew exactly where Jesus was standing, even though he had no visual sense of this. Our prompting should be as gentle and non-suggestive as possible, but we probably do need to prompt. It is gentle prompting that encourages people to explore and own the presence of Jesus. Without prompting, most people will probably focus on what they are not experiencing rather than on what they are. The way that I usually prompt people to engage with Jesus' presence is to simply ask, 'Where would you say Jesus is for you right now?' Sometimes it might be helpful to give suggestions that allow them to own what they are feeling. The more suggestions we can give, the less pressurised people will feel to choose the one that they feel they are expected to choose: 'Is he beside you, in front of you, within you, around you, in a different place?' Again, there is no suggestion that they should answer in any particular way, nor that they should conjure up a mental picture of what Jesus looks like.

I have seen some beautiful things happening when people are encouraged to take Jesus' presence seriously.

I was encouraging one group of about ten people to find his presence, and as I watched one lady across the room, I saw her change from standing upright to leaning her head right over to the side. When I asked her what she was doing, she shared that she could sense Jesus standing right by her side and she was leaning her head on his shoulder.

I watched another lady in a similar group setting, and as I encouraged the group to find the presence of Jesus, she wrapped her arms in an embrace around the Jesus she could experience before her.

I have also seen people reach out to take the hand of Jesus. Sometimes they turn to the side as they experience his presence in a very definite location.

When we are leading people in a time of encountering Jesus, we also need to stand back to allow him to be continually refreshing in the way that he ministers to people.

On one occasion I was leading a time of ministry to the whole congregation in a church. Afterwards, a lady shared how she had sensed Jesus high up in the church looking down on her.

After a few minutes I led her in another time of encounter and on this occasion, only a short while later, her sense of the presence of Jesus was quite different; he was right in front of her. Neither experience was better than the other, he simply wanted to show her something different.

A common question asked is what if people are unable to find his presence in any way. Simply saying, 'Don't worry!' probably won't offer much in the way of comfort. My reaction to those (actually quite a small number) who are unable to experience Jesus in this way is to sit down with them and talk about what they did experience. What I often find is that some people will say they didn't experience anything, all they felt was peace. This is actually quite a profound experience. So many people would pay a fortune to experience peace. I encourage those who experience this to view it as the presence of Jesus for them. When Isaiah looks forward to the coming Messiah (Isaiah 9:6), one of the titles that he gives him is 'Prince of Peace'. It is only natural that when the Prince of Peace comes near to someone they experience something of his peace.

Commenting on her experience at one of our teaching days, someone emailed us with this: 'In the last session, when you invited us to focus on the presence of Jesus, I was troubled that I could not find him anywhere, I could not sense his presence at all. But I was aware of the Holy Spirit reminding me of the areas in my life that need refining. I have a critical spirit and feel I easily wound people by my tongue; I have been working on it but still find myself doing it. As I thought about this, I realised where Jesus was . . . he was in my mind! He was helping me to change and take on Christ's attributes! Praise him! Since Saturday I feel I have been enabled to

> *pray more freely, my imagination has been enhanced and I can sense better what God is saying to me! I feel I speak more softly and wisely and I pray God can use me more, even more.'*

Sometimes this is such a new thing for people to grasp that it may well take them two or three times of encountering Jesus before they relax into the possibility of Jesus coming to them in such a way.

If, for some reason, someone finds it impossible to be in the presence of Jesus, it may prove helpful to use the Bible as a way of helping them experience Jesus' presence. Read a story, encourage them to find themselves in that story and to work out where they are in relation to Jesus, and then encourage them to move on to have a conversation with him. When we do this for ourselves, it is far easier to go at a pace that suits us – we know when to move on – so there may be a temptation to rush people through this, as we are fearful that they are waiting for us to 'get on with it'. Another temptation will always be to use too many words, as we feel that they may be uncomfortable with silence.

When we pray with people, our desire is naturally to take their requests and turn them into prayers. What we are discovering at The Christian Healing Mission is that even when people share their concerns with us, those concerns might not be what are actually on their hearts. We may only find this out when people stand in the presence of God.

> *I remember one lady sharing her particular prayer concern, which was a painful physical condition. As we came to the time of prayer, I led her in the simple 'Father, Son, Spirit'*

approach. What was fascinating and so moving was that when she found the presence of Jesus, he was enthroned in heaven, and when prompted to speak to him, what came out of her mouth was a beautiful declaration of love and worship. It was as if her previous prayer concern was forgotten as she stood in the presence of God.

Sometimes people do want to speak out their concerns to Jesus, and they are no less holy for doing so. When Jesus asked Bartimaeus what he could do for him (Mark 10:51), he was probably not expecting Bartimaeus to say anything other than express his desire to see. What is also fascinating is that when people express their desires to Jesus, they do so with a clarity and succinctness that is not possible when they are sharing with other people. It is as if they know that he knows, and they do not have to express every nuance or put everything in its context. They are standing before the one who knows everything.

They are standing before the one who knows everything

The 'next stage' is to encourage them to listen to Jesus themselves and hear his voice speaking to them. Some people may need encouragement to believe that this really is Jesus communicating with them. They may feel that they are simply making it up or that what is coming to them is wishful thinking. I often encourage people to share out loud what Jesus says or shows them, as this helps them to own it in a way that they may not if they keep it to themselves.

This part of the process need not be simply a one-line statement from the person about what God is saying – they may need to explore what they sense he is sharing with them. It may be that what Jesus says to them is totally unexpected, or they find themselves with a picture they cannot understand. Bring the person back to that sense of the presence of Jesus and encourage them to have a conversation with him about whatever it is that they do not understand. The temptation is always for us to offer our own interpretation (which indeed may be the correct one) but it will mean so much more if they hear it from Jesus.

One of the most crucial things we need to be aware of at this time is being open to Jesus' agenda. We would all love to see more healing, but perhaps one of the reasons why we do not is because we are seeking to pursue our own agenda rather than seeking to follow his. It does require a certain discipline on our part to stand with the person in their own journey with Jesus as he shares his heart with them, rather than imposing anything upon them that might actually be a distraction from what he is seeking to do at that particular time.

> **. . . stand with the person in their own journey with Jesus as he shares his heart with them**

After a weekend visit to a church, we received a letter:

> *Four weeks ago, when I went for prayer, it was suggested that I consider where Jesus might be for me at that point. I soon 'saw' him at the roadside with a crowd of people gathered around him. I was standing at a distance on my own, wishing I could join in. Then Jesus looked towards me and said, 'Why do you always wait for me to come to you? Why don't you come to me?' This spoke to me, as I realised it was true – not only with Jesus, but also with other people.*

> *Now, being prayed for again, I found myself as a child playing hide-and-seek with Jesus. 'Do you really want to find me?' he called. Yes, I did, so I chased around until I found him and was lifted off my feet and swung around with much joy. The verse that popped into my mind was 'You will seek me and find me when you seek me with all your heart' (Jeremiah 29:13).*

2. Faith

Before we move on to consider the third 'spotlight', the role of the Holy Spirit as we pray for someone, pause for a moment to reflect again that we are resting in God's presence. As we begin to focus on his greatness and all that his presence implies, our faith is likely to grow. Faith is something that is very much associated with Christian healing. There is, from what Jesus said, evidently a connection between faith and healing:

> *I have not found anyone in Israel with such great faith.* (Matthew 8:10)

> *When Jesus saw their faith, he said to the [paralysed] man, 'Take heart, son; your sins are forgiven.'* (Matthew 9:2)

> *Your faith has healed you.* (Matthew 9:22)

The problem is that it is so easy to think that faith is a barrier over which we must jump, and if we do not have enough of it then how can we expect healing to happen? We are going to look at a number of questions regarding faith, beginning with looking at what faith is, who it is who should be having faith and then looking at ways in which we can increase our faith.

What is faith?

Perhaps the most illuminating passage about the nature of faith in the Bible is to be found in Mark 11:12–24. The passage naturally falls into three sections:

Verses 12–14

The next day as they were leaving Bethany, Jesus was hungry. Seeing in the distance a fig-tree in leaf, he went to find out if it had any fruit. When he reached it, he found nothing but leaves, because it was not the season for figs. Then he said to the tree, 'May no one ever eat fruit from you again.' And his disciples heard him say it.

Verses 15–19

On reaching Jerusalem, Jesus entered the temple courts and began driving out those who were buying and selling there. He overturned the tables of the money-changers and the benches of those selling doves, and would not allow anyone to carry merchandise through the temple courts. And as he taught them, he said, 'Is it not written: "My house will be called a house of prayer for all nations"? But you have made it "a den of robbers".' The chief priests and the teachers of the law heard this and began looking for a way to kill him, for they feared him, because the whole crowd was amazed at his teaching. When evening came, they went out of the city.

Verses 20–24

In the morning, as they went along, they saw the fig-tree withered from the roots. Peter remembered and said to Jesus, 'Rabbi, look! The fig-tree you cursed has withered!' 'Have faith in God,' Jesus answered. 'Truly I tell you, if anyone says to this mountain, "Go, throw yourself into the sea," and does not doubt in their heart but believes that what they say will happen, it will be done for them. Therefore I tell you, whatever you ask for in prayer, believe that you have received it, and it will be yours.'

The passage begins with a frustrating lunchtime! We read in verses 12–14 that Jesus was hungry and went to a fig tree to get some fruit. Discovering that the tree had no fruit on it, Jesus cursed the fig tree. To add to the strangeness of the story, we read that it would have been surprising if there had been figs on the tree, as this was not the season for figs anyway. It sounds a bit like complaining that your favourite restaurant is not open at four o'clock in the morning when you decide you want to eat!

The second part of the story occurs in verses 15–19, when Jesus went to the Temple and was distressed at its lack of prayer – it, too, seemed like a barren fig tree and he acted to cleanse it.

The third part of the narrative is what seems to give us some insight into the incident of the fig tree, for in verses 20–24 Jesus and his disciples go back to the (now withered) fig tree and Jesus uses the incident to teach. Interestingly, he doesn't teach about the state of the Temple. Rather, the lessons he draws from the fig tree are lessons about the nature of faith and what faith looks like in practice. In these verses he gives us an insight into how he prayed for things (presumably whether they were fig trees or people who were sick). What seems to be emphasised in this third, final passage is this:

Whatever you ask for in prayer, believe that you have received it, and it will be yours.

What Jesus seems to be sharing is that when he prayed for people or events, he had an ability to be able to see it as something already given.

Whose faith are we talking about?

In Matthew 17, Jesus and his close disciples experienced the wonder of the Transfiguration. When they came down the mountain, they discovered that a 'ministry session' was not going well; the remaining disciples were unable to do what was being asked of them – namely to cast a spirit out of a boy. Jesus took over and a wonderful healing happened. Later, when the disciples asked him why it worked for him and not for them, he said: 'Because you have so little faith' (Matthew 17:20). Jesus was not questioning the faith of the boy, or his father, but rather those who were doing the praying – the prayer ministers.

Of course, it is good to encourage the faith of those coming for prayer, but it is interesting to note that certainly in Matthew 17 it is the faith of those doing the ministry that is the cause of the boy not receiving healing.

On another occasion, Jesus was making his way to the house of the synagogue ruler, Jairus, to heal his daughter (Mark 5:21–43). On the way, Jesus was interrupted by a woman who was longing to be healed. Jesus gave such time and care to her that in the meantime Jairus' daughter died. Undeterred, Jesus carried on to Jairus' house, saying to Jairus: 'Don't be afraid; just believe' (Mark 5:36). Why did he say that? Was it simply to reassure him, or is it possible that Jesus needed something to grow within Jairus as he approached the dead girl?

On yet another occasion, in Matthew 9, Jesus was approached by two blind men and his question to them was, 'Do you believe that I am able to do this?' What was the reason for this question? Was it just to discover if they could give the right answer to his question? Perhaps what he was seeking to do was to encourage them in their faith, to invite them to ponder the question so that faith would grow within them.

So in reply to the question, 'Whose faith are we talking about?' the answer is not entirely clear cut. Faith is evidently important in the process of healing, but it may be found in any one of the different people involved. Perhaps the source of the faith doesn't seem to matter as long as it is present somewhere.

How can we increase our faith?

Jesus was both fully God and fully man, and it is tempting to think that in the moments when he exercised great power he was acting out of his divinity. The trouble with that view is that when he calls us to share in this ministry, how can he expect us humans to do what he did as God?

Evidently there is a difference between Jesus and us. He had knowledge of who he was and the power available to him in a way that surpasses our knowledge and awareness. Our faith is based not so much on that knowledge, but rather on our trust in the truths about Jesus. In John 14:12, Jesus said, 'Whoever believes in me will do the works I have been doing, and they will do even greater things than these, because I am going to the Father.' In other words, any ministry of healing today is not just based on the love of God that Jesus demonstrated in his ministry when he walked the earth; it is based on the glorious truths of his death, resurrection and ascension. The object of our faith may be different, but the nature of faith is the same. It is still that ability to be able to see something from a different perspective.

In our quest to grow our faith, it might be helpful for us to remind ourselves of four great truths about the Jesus in whose presence we stand. One way of looking at these is to phrase them as four simple questions:

- What does God think of me, or of the person for whom I am praying?

- What does God want?

- What has God already done?

- How can I find more?

To pose these questions is to actively engage with an answer, and it forces us to engage with God's heart for us.

What does God think of us?

Of course, the answer is that he loves us. We can say with confidence that God loves us. We are not talking about an emotion, but rather a love that compels action. This is what is behind some of the most well-known words of the Bible, such as John 3:16: 'For God so loved the world that he gave his one and only Son.' Every time we see an image of Jesus, or an image of the cross, it can serve as a reminder of the nature of the love of God who sent Jesus to us; God's love for us compelled Jesus to come for us. Paul writes in Galatians 2:20, 'the Son of God, who loved me and gave himself for me'. Just as it is not an emotion, nor is it a love that judges; rather, it is a love that is longing to reach out and save. John 3 continues, 'For God did not send his Son into the world to condemn the world, but to save the world through him' (v17). In other words, when we bring ourselves to God, we can have that certainty that we are utterly loved by him with a love that has no hint of condemnation and a love that was utterly self-sacrificing for us. This is not just about the general love of God for the world, but his active love for each of us personally. Yes, God loves the world and gave Jesus for the world, but he also loves us and gave Jesus for each one of us.

When we are praying for others, faith is lifted by us audibly thanking God for his unique, real and practical love for this person. It is good to take as much time as you need to let your heart, and the heart of the one for whom you are praying, be filled with a confidence about the heart of God for them.

What does God want, either for us, or for those for whom we pray?

Perhaps one of the most significant moments in the life of Jesus occurred at the very beginning of his public ministry. In Luke 4:14–30, Jesus goes to his home town of Nazareth and enters the synagogue, where he is invited to preach. He begins by choosing a passage from Isaiah 61:1–2 which he reads aloud:

The Spirit of the Lord is on me, because he has anointed me to proclaim good news to the poor. He has sent me to proclaim freedom for the prisoners and recovery of sight for the blind, to set the oppressed free, to proclaim the year of the Lord's favour. (Luke 4:18–19)

Then he rolled up the scroll, gave it back to the attendant and sat down. The eyes of everyone in the synagogue were fastened on him. He began by saying to them, 'Today this scripture is fulfilled in your hearing.' (Luke 4:20–21)

What Jesus is saying is that these words from Isaiah apply to him. They are about him, they summarise his mission and this is what people can expect from him.

His mission is good news to the poor

This might well be a general opening statement which summarises the claims that follow. In general terms, poverty is all about what we lack; it is about what we are unable to do for ourselves. For example, Jesus goes on to talk about freedom for prisoners. Prisoners are people whose poverty is expressed in their lack of freedom. He goes on to talk about those who are sick; their poverty can be perceived in the health that they lack. For those who are oppressed, their poverty is in the lack of freedom from those things that weigh them down. With God, however, whatever we do not have is not the end of the matter – we have him, who has been revealed as the provider, our peace and our healer.

His mission is freedom for the prisoners

Leaving aside questions of false imprisonment, a prisoner is someone who is being punished for what he has done wrong. We may go through hardships in our lives, some of which are no doubt undeserved and unfair, but likely as not there will be some aspects of our hardships that we deserve. The world says something along the lines of, 'You've made your bed, now lie on it'; but the words of Jesus are quite different. He says, 'Take up your bed and walk!' To those who have sinned, the message of Jesus is stunning – there is forgiveness and a new start. There was something amazing about Jesus in that his holiness did not seem to repel sinners, but rather attract them to him. It is tempting to think that we cannot come to Jesus until we are clean, but this is simply not true; we come to him first and then find his forgiveness.

His mission is recovery of sight for the blind

It is tempting to explain this in terms of the new vision that Jesus gives us as Christians, but healing was something that Jesus took very seriously. In his brief time of ministry on earth, a significant amount of the gospel stories describe Jesus healing those people who were sick.

His mission is release for the oppressed

Perhaps this statement refers to those who are suffering as a result of others. All too often our suffering is a result of what others do to us. Words that people speak can stick to us for a long time, or their actions can bruise us. Sometimes it comes down to what we experienced in our upbringing, whether conscious hurt was intended or not, and we find ourselves not functioning as well as we would like.

> *I was once speaking to a group of young teenagers, and after I had shared a little about encountering Jesus I invited them to find that sense of his presence. As I spoke to one boy, he shared how he found it difficult to relate to people of his own age. After a lovely time of encountering Jesus, he shared how chains were falling from his heart onto the floor.*

This mission of Jesus is an outworking of God's desire to bless us. We have already looked at the blessing that God commanded Aaron to use in Numbers 6, and when we look at the statement in Luke 4 it really answers the question of just how much does God want to bless us.

Perhaps all of this can be summed up in John 10:10, where Jesus says, 'I have come that they may have life, and have it to the full.' These words are actually part of a very beautiful passage which begins in the previous account of when Jesus healed a man born blind. That healing miracle led to a discussion with the Pharisees about who Jesus really was. There was a break in the discussion as the Pharisees threw the healed man out of the synagogue. Jesus went in search of him and found him, and his discussion with the Pharisees picked up again at that point. Jesus went on to speak about his role as the one through whom people can find God, and identified himself as the gateway to the fold, and indeed as the good shepherd himself. It is in this context that Jesus looked round and, probably referring to the crowd that was gathering, announced that he had come 'that they may have life, and have it to the full'. What is fullness of life, or abundant life? Does this necessarily mean that Jesus wants to bring healing? Jesus contrasts the abundant life that he came to bring with the work of the devil, who came 'to steal and kill and destroy' (verse 10). The mission of Jesus is to restore what has been taken from us and his ministry of healing can certainly be seen in that light.

> **The mission of Jesus is to restore what has been taken from us**

Similarly, when Jesus referred to himself as the good shepherd, he did so in the context of a discussion with the Pharisees and it seems likely that he had a specific passage in mind – Ezekiel 34, where good and bad leaders of the people are compared to good and bad shepherds of the flock. One of the accusations against the bad shepherds is that they have not 'healed those who are ill' (Ezekiel 34:4). The promise of the good shepherd in Ezekiel 34:16 is that he will 'bind up the injured'. This is the ministry of the good shepherd: he cares for his sheep, and when we come to him as broken and wounded people, he will care for us and bind us up.

When we are praying for others, it is a matter of finding the answer to our original question – 'What does God want for this person?' – and expressing it so that our confidence, and that of the person for whom we are praying, will grow. The truth is that Jesus' desire for this person is that they have abundant life. That is what he wants for the whole world; he said that was why he came (John 10:10). So that must be his desire for every person for whom we pray. The question we have to ask ourselves is whether we believe that Jesus still shares that same mission today as he did then. Certainly he saw that mission continuing past his death. In the final meal he shared with his followers, he made the dramatic statement we have already explored in John 14:12:

Very truly I tell you, whoever believes in me will do the works I have been doing, and they will do even greater things than these, because I am going to the Father.

When we encounter Jesus today, this is who we meet. The mission that governed his life then is still his mission for us today. Of course, he may have his own agenda as to how that mission is to be realised in our lives, but our encounters are with the Jesus who loves us and who is committed to our transformation.

We catch more of his desire for healing in a story that appears in Mark 3:1–5:

Another time Jesus went into the synagogue, and a man with a shrivelled hand was there. Some of them were looking for a reason to accuse Jesus, so they watched him closely to see if he would heal him on the Sabbath. Jesus said to the man with the shrivelled hand, 'Stand up in front of everyone.' Then Jesus asked them, 'Which is lawful on the Sabbath: to do good or to do evil, to save life or to kill?' But they remained silent. He looked around at them in anger and, deeply distressed at their stubborn hearts, said to the man, 'Stretch out your hand.' He stretched it out, and his hand was completely restored.

What is most fascinating about this story is what it reveals about the heart of Jesus when it comes to the question of healing. Some of those present in the synagogue felt that it was inappropriate to heal on the Sabbath, so they were looking to see what Jesus was going to do next. Of course Jesus did heal the man, but it is his motives for doing so that are particularly interesting. These were revealed in his question, 'Which is lawful on the Sabbath: to do good or to do evil, to save life or to kill?'

Jesus didn't seem to offer any middle ground in what he said: healing was regarded as doing good and denying healing as doing evil. This might seem quite a challenging attitude compared to how we often think about healing. It is so tempting to assume that God makes a decision to heal some people but, for reasons unknown to us, decides not to heal others. Yet what this passage shows with simple clarity is that God cannot take any delight in our sicknesses, nor can he be seen to be denying healing, as by the admission of Jesus this would make him evil.

Surely this must boost our confidence in praying to God? If we take these words seriously, then no longer are we praying to a God who may or may not want to heal, but rather to a God who must want to heal, simply because he is a good God. No longer do we have to end our prayers with the words 'if it be your will', because the heart of our good God has already been revealed as a God who longs to heal. We will look at some of the reasons why healing may not happen a little later, but it is not about what God does or does not want to do.

What has God already done for us?

Jesus' healing ministry was a central part of his work; taking away sickness and infirmity was not a minor task. People debate the place of the cross in his healing ministry – did he die for our sicknesses as well as our sins? The outcome of this debate is whether we can expect healing to happen because Jesus died on the cross in the same way that we can expect sin to be forgiven?

We have looked at the verse from John 14:12, 'Very truly I tell you, whoever believes in me will do the works I have been doing, and they will do even greater things than these, because I am going to the Father.' It does seem that Jesus saw a link between the ministry that believers would exercise and his death, resurrection and ascension. It is therefore certainly true that healing flows through the death of Jesus. Without his death, there would be no healing ministry or any aspect of the Lord's ministry today. While Jesus stated in John 10:10 that he came that we might have life and have it to the full, it is interesting that in the next verse he declared, 'I am the good shepherd. The good shepherd lays down his life for the sheep.' He gave his life for our total transformation, and healing is part of that transformation. It is certainly his pleasure and desire that we call out to him for healing for what might be seen as individual sicknesses, but it is also true that he may desire to do other things in our lives before, after, as well as, or alongside bringing healing for those particular ailments. His desire is to heal every part of us. Our problem is that we can become fixated on him healing the area that we want to be healed.

His desire is to heal every part of us

How can I find more?

If all that we have said is true, then how can we find what flows as a result of these truths? Hebrews 4:16 is an inspiring verse:

Let us approach God's throne of grace with confidence, so that we may receive mercy and find grace to help us in our time of need.

The confidence that we are encouraged to find is what should be growing within us as we consider the previous three questions: because he loves us, because his desire is to bring healing and because he gave his life that we might have abundant life, we can come to him knowing that we are not asking for something outside of his will, nor will he reject us in any way. We can also be confident that whatever we receive flows from his grace and mercy and not from what we think we do or do not deserve.

A simple prayer is to ask the Holy Spirit to bring you the power of God to touch your situation.

Dwelling on these four truths can greatly grow our faith, and can have the effect of opening up the heart of the person for whom we are praying without us having to promise what we cannot deliver, and without us making claims that may well end in disappointment. What we are seeking to do is to change the focus of

What we are seeking to do is to change the focus of prayer

prayer. What happens when we begin to focus on the revelation of Jesus is that we take our eyes off the enormity of the problem and fix them on something bigger.

Practising your faith

We have looked before at the practice of holding a cross when we are praying as a way of keeping our attention focused. You might find it helpful to hold a cross for this exercise.

As you hold the top 'arm', begin to worship Jesus as the revelation of the love of God. Worship the Father for his love for you, a love that compelled him to send Jesus for you. Worship Jesus for his willingness to come to this earth for you and to die for you. Let it become as personal as it can be.

Move to the second 'arm', and begin to worship Jesus for his mission of transformation. He came to bring fullness of life to you. Take a moment to consider those parts of your life where you would say that fullness is lacking, areas where you long to see his touch. Don't keep the focus on those things, but return to the wonder of his promise to transform.

Hold onto the third arm and worship Jesus who laid down his life that you might have abundant life. Rejoice in prayer that Jesus has done everything to release abundant life into those areas of your life that need his touch.

Finally, as you hold the final arm of the cross, be confident before him and ask him to bring his Holy Spirit to release his mercy and grace to you.

3. Power

When we were looking at the person of the Holy Spirit towards the end of Part 2, we noted how it is the Holy Spirit who brings us the good things of God. Now we are going to look a little more at this, and in particular at how he brings the power of God to us in the context of the healing ministry.

In most of the gospel stories about healing, there comes a moment when there seems to be a release of power from Jesus to the sufferer. We see this release of power happening in various ways, either by a word being spoken or by touch, or sometimes both. For example:

> *Jesus reached out his hand and touched the man . . . 'Be clean!'* (Matthew 8:3)

> *He touched her hand and the fever left her.* (Matthew 8:15)

At one of our meetings, a young mum had a profound experience of God. I asked her to give her own account of what happened:

> *I was 28 when it happened. I had had problems with my hips since I was pregnant with my second son (four years earlier). It was so bad I was on strong pain killers that I couldn't take in the long term, as they would start to cause problems with my stomach. I found it difficult to get up the stairs in my own home and a walk that used to take three minutes would take fifteen. I felt I couldn't look after my children and it was having a detrimental effect on my marriage.*
>
> *At the end of the first healing session while we were praying, I asked if God would allow me to be able to do his work, but*

I couldn't concentrate because I couldn't stop shaking from the waist down. I remember thinking, 'I wish this shaking would stop, I can't concentrate on praying.' Then my mobile phone started to vibrate so I rushed to turn it off! As I did, the prayers ended. As I started to move out of the pew I realised I had no pain in my right hip! I couldn't stop laughing!

After the second teaching session we prayed again. This time I said to God, 'OK, God, I'm really grateful you've healed my right hip, but what about the other one?' As I finished saying that my whole body started shaking, up my arms at first and then my legs kept giving way a little. I had a big urge to laugh out loud, but I didn't! At the end of the prayers it was time for lunch. As I turned with a big grin on my face, my husband and children (aged six and nearly four), were coming into church to meet me. I bounced out of the pew and ran to them, as God had blessed me with complete healing! My husband's jaw dropped! We truly have an Awesome God! Now I really am able to do God's work! I'm blessed to work with women with postnatal depression, and my husband and I are leading a home group in our local church, which I wouldn't have been able to do beforehand as I couldn't even drive the car or tidy my house!

It is this element of the healing ministry that is often the most challenging. We may feel certain that Jesus is with us, and we can spend time meditating on the Scriptures and see our faith grow, but when it comes to praying for our healing or laying our hands on the sick and actually having the faith to see healing, it seems that it is either going to happen or not – there isn't much we can do about it.

One of the most fascinating passages about power in the New Testament occurs in Ephesians 1:18–19. In this passage, Paul shares with the Ephesians a prayer that is on his heart. His prayer begins, 'I pray that the eyes of your heart may be enlightened in order that you may know . . .'

Paul then goes on to share three things that he hopes will happen as the eyes of the hearts of the Ephesians are opened: that they would know hope; that they would have an understanding of the riches of inheritance; and that they might know 'his incomparably great power for us who believe'. It is this third element that is most interesting.

It is worth noting two things at this stage. First, Paul was not praying that the Ephesians would receive any more power, but rather that their eyes would be opened to what was already there. In other words, they had this power already. Their problem was that they did not know they had it. The second interesting point that Paul makes is that this power is for those who believe. In other words, this was not something that was unique to the Ephesian church, but rather it is a truth in which all believers can share. Power is there for all of us.

Power is there for all of us

What can we expect this power to be like? Paul goes on to write, 'That power is the same as the mighty strength he exerted when he raised Christ from the dead.' Our confusion in all of this is that frankly we don't feel as if that power is there. On some occasions we may feel something, but most of the time we do not. One would think at the very least that we would feel something akin to electricity flowing through us as we receive the power of God for ourselves, or as we laid hands on the sick. We read what Paul says is there, and yet our feelings tell us that it isn't. What are we meant to do?

It probably comes back to a simple question of faith again. Dare we believe that such power is available to us? Dare we ask God to open the eyes of our hearts so that we may know this power that is there?

A starting place to receive the power of God is to ask the Holy Spirit to come upon us, or upon those to whom we are ministering, and to bring the reality of God's power to us. The Spirit of God is of course already so near to us – our physical bodies are temples designed to bear his presence. When we ask the Holy Spirit to come to us or others, it is like shorthand for a number of prayers:

- a renewed sense of his presence

- a surrendering of more of us to more of him

- the touch of his power upon our need.

Our prayer is not that the Holy Spirit will come where he may otherwise be absent, but rather for a deeper touch, that we may yield more to his presence. Yet the encouragement is that this power is there and it is available for us who believe. It is interesting that when the Holy Spirit comes, this is sometimes accompanied by physical manifestations. People may shake, fall, cry, their breathing pattern might change or their eyelids might flicker. Whether it is the Spirit producing these manifestations, or whether these are ways in which human bodies sometimes react to the presence of something other than themselves, is unclear. However, it is important to stress that any absence of manifestations is not to say that the Spirit is not powerfully present. Different people react to things in various ways, and the way we react to the presence of God is no different. The promise of Jesus is that the Spirit will come when asked.

If you then, though you are evil, know how to give good gifts to your children, how much more will your Father in heaven give the Holy Spirit to those who ask him! (Luke 11:13)

When we sense the presence of the Spirit, perhaps the best thing we can do is to wait and let him do whatever he wants to do. There is often the temptation to pray with many words. Our actual words can be few as we pray – as the words of Jesus certainly were when he prayed.

When we are with someone and praying for them, the second thing that can help is what we often formally call 'the laying on of hands'. It can be as simple as laying a hand upon someone's shoulder as we pray for them (with their permission). This gift of touch, or laying on of hands, is a living sign that it is not our words or our wisdom that are going to make any difference to them. What is needed is the power of God to bring healing. This is what touch conveys. It is the Spirit within us that flows through us into them. Paul writes in Romans 8:11, 'The Spirit of him who raised Jesus from the dead is living in you.' This is the basis for our

It is the Spirit within us that flows through us into them

confidence as we touch someone in the name of Jesus, so that the Spirit within us will indeed flow through us to bring his change to them. For this reason, the words we use can be few. It is not the length of our spoken prayers that will make a difference. The power of the Spirit flowing in silence can be very powerful as we faithfully believe in what he is doing through us.

Ever since I was in my late teens I have suffered from a bad back, so it was no surprise when recently I was bent almost double again. Instead of seeking medical help, I continued at work for the next two months or so. I commute to and from work by car and sit at a desk all day, tapping on a laptop. The pain and discomfort in my back increased, but I felt I shouldn't take time off. In the end I went to see my GP. 'Off work immediately,' she said. The pain got worse and I had to cancel a holiday as I could not even get to the airport. Then the problem developed into sciatica. Although I felt pretty low from time to time, a cocktail of drugs reduced the pain along with physiotherapy.

During this difficult time my wife suggested that I visit The Healing Mission (CHM). And so it was that I attended a couple of services, which led to one particular encounter.

You never really know what God has in mind for you, do you? At a previous service we had been told that if we didn't think God had healed the specific thing we wanted healing for, he would have been healing something else, as that is his nature. With that in mind, I attended this particular healing service with an open mind. 'Whatever you want, Lord, but healing the back would be great,' was my approach. As I write, I'm ashamed to say that I can't specifically recall the Bible passage, but I do remember being encouraged to be aware that it is sometimes us who can get in the way of God doing what he wants to do. The prayers invited and encouraged me to seek to meet with Jesus . . . and I did.

As a child, my parents repeatedly took me to Cornwall for our summer holidays (I am an only child). These were always happy times. Rocks skirted the beach and we would set up camp each morning around a particular rock. This rock was so big that it remained unmoved for all of those summer holidays, and this is the place where I met with Jesus. He was sitting on the rock half-turned towards me, sometimes looking out to sea, sometimes glancing around the small, horseshoe bay. As I stood not far from him, our eyes met and he told me that he was going to heal me – to touch me himself, to heal me himself. With a gesture of his hand, he invited me to sit next to him. I found I couldn't move. I could not approach my Lord. Why not? I had just been invited to receive healing. Healing was what I had come here for. Healing was what I wanted. Healing was what I needed. What was preventing me from accepting this amazing invitation? Amidst my confusion and uncertainty, I could still hear the prayers to this loving Jesus, and for healing. Jesus remained on the rock. He waited. He was patient. His expression was loving, gentle and kind. Suddenly I realised what was holding me back: fear. Fear that if I accepted this extraordinary and personal invitation, I might experience failure – a failure to be healed either because this whole experience was a creation of my own, or because if I was physically touched by Jesus and was not completely healed physically then I would have let him down. Of course, none of this necessarily makes sense, but those were my predominant thoughts.

Then I had a real sense that I was being very silly. Jesus didn't need to touch me to heal me; he could do that through someone else or from miles away. I realised that Jesus was merely inviting me to come and sit with him on the rock and during that time he was going to heal me. The barrier – physical, psychological, stupid, call it what you like – came tumbling down and I walked, as easy as anything, to the rock and sat down next to Jesus. We sat next to each other and looked out to sea; no words were necessary. Then, quietly, he pointed out to me that our hips (at that particular time my right hip was problematic) were touching, and our legs were touching. He didn't need to touch me with his hand to heal me; the process had begun without my knowing it. I almost burst out laughing at my naivety! Jesus repeated that he intended to heal me. I was overcome with a rainbow of emotions, joy and awe being those I recall most clearly.

I did not leave CHM that day running like an athlete, but I did know that I would be healed – in Jesus' time. And so I am being healed, both physically and in other areas of my life, which, because I have had more time to spend with God during this period in my life, he has addressed. So many lessons learned and still to learn! Thank you, Lord.

15
NO GUARANTEES

I am not suggesting that simply following certain steps will automatically bring healing. It is God who brings healing, not any formula or pattern that we follow. Our God is a living God, not a slot machine. Indeed, one of the dangers of following any pattern is that we can begin to pay more attention to this than to the living God, and at that moment we need to find again for ourselves that wonderful sense of his presence.

Instead, what we have been exploring is that when Jesus ministers to us he may well have his own agenda for how he brings about his transformation of our bodies, minds and spirits. For that reason we cannot make any guarantees about what God will or will not do as we come into his presence.

This makes praying for healing a sensitive matter as we try to hold on to the faith that Jesus encourages yet without being presumptive. There will be many times when Christ-like and faith-filled Christians face disappointment when prayers are seemingly not answered. This raises one of the most common questions about healing: why is it that many people are not healed? Our basic premise is that the same Jesus who ministered on earth is with us now, so why don't we see the healing today that he saw then?

One thing worth bearing in mind is that even in the ministry of Jesus, not all the healing stories are as straight forward as we might imagine. At times he seems to set out a different agenda for somebody's healing. This can be seen in the story that we have already touched on where the four friends brought their paralysed companion to Jesus. Mark 2:1–12 recounts how the four men couldn't get their friend anywhere near Jesus, so they climbed up onto the roof, dug through it and lowered their friend down through the hole so that he was right in front of Jesus. In verse 5 we read something strange: 'When Jesus saw their faith, he said to the paralysed man, "Son, your sins are forgiven."' This man was evidently unable to walk, but the first thing Jesus did was not to heal the man's legs, but to speak about forgiveness. The four friends certainly had their own agenda about what they wanted to happen, and the paralysed man probably knew what he wanted to happen, but Jesus did something completely different. He went on to heal the man's physical condition a little later in the story, but he had a different priority.

Another example of this can be seen in John 11 in the story of the raising of Lazarus from the dead. In verse 3 we are told that the sisters sent word to Jesus saying, 'Lord, the one you love is ill.' Their agenda is quite plain and quite natural – they wanted Jesus to come and heal their brother. We might expect from reading other healing stories in the gospels that Jesus would go and do just that. However, we see Jesus pursuing a different agenda in this case. He deliberately waits where he is (verse 6) as Lazarus gets worse and then dies. Jesus' agenda was to raise Lazarus from the dead, not to heal his ailing body.

. . . we are too set on pursuing our own agendas rather than giving Jesus the chance to reveal his to us

One of the main reasons why we don't see as much healing as we would like is probably because we are too set on pursuing our own agendas rather than giving Jesus the chance to reveal his to us.

On one occasion we were leading a healing service, and a lady wrote to us afterwards explaining that she had not been healed at the service. She wrote, 'I came to last night's service seeking something and what I came away with was far above my hopes and expectations. It was during the meditative part of your healing service that I was once again brought into the very presence of Jesus. You asked for people to come forwards for prayer and to share with the prayer ministry team what it was that Jesus had said to us. I declined this offer, and neither did I put my hand up. My reason was that I was just so wrapped up in the arms of Jesus, which is where he wanted me to be.'

Her agenda in coming to the service was that God would heal her back, but God had his own agenda in wanting to wrap her in the sense of his love. Perhaps this reveals something about the way that we define healing. It is tempting to think of healing as God answering our prayers that we might get better. Actually, healing is about the transformation of our bodies, minds and spirits. The lady who wrote to us after the healing service did experience healing, just not in the way she thought she wanted, though the touch of God upon her was real.

On another occasion we were with a church and a man asked for prayer for a physical condition. As we began to go through the simple steps of encounter prayer, this man found the presence of Jesus and expressed his desire that Jesus would heal him. When I asked what Jesus was showing him, he said he had a picture of his friend with whom he had argued some weeks previously. When we talked about what this might mean, he concluded that on this occasion Jesus' agenda was that he found peace with his friend before anything else would happen.

So what confidence can we have when we pray? Does Jesus want to heal us? Is there no guarantee?

In John 6:40, Jesus says, 'For my Father's will is that everyone who looks to the Son and believes in him shall have eternal life.' In this statement, Jesus clearly sets out what God desperately wants for all of us – eternal life. Furthermore, later in the same gospel (John 17:3) Jesus reveals the nature of eternal life, which is far from simply being something that happens when we die: 'Now this is eternal life: that they know you, the only true God, and Jesus Christ, whom you have sent.' Eternal life is about relationship with God. This is what we can guarantee that the Father wants for every person. Our relationship with Jesus is, as Luke 4:18–19 reveals, to bring transformation to us. It is not that we have to reach a certain level of relationship with God in order to get healed, but rather that as our relationship with God opens up, healing begins.

. . . as our relationship with God opens up, healing begins

> *A lady shared her experience. She said, 'Jesus was standing there and seemed a terribly ordinary person. He wasn't in robes and didn't appear to be an Israeli; dare I say it, he seemed English! He gripped my arms and when I asked for healing, he said, "First things first – I want you to know how much I love you." That's so relevant to what I am going through and reading about at the moment. That's the focus and not the healing.'*

The other aspect of this ministry over which we have no guarantee is God's timing. Jesus told a helpful parable in Mark 4:26–29:

> *This is what the kingdom of God is like. A man scatters seed on the ground. Night and day, whether he sleeps or gets up, the seed sprouts and grows, though he does not know how. All by itself the soil produces corn – first the stalk, then the ear, then the full grain in the ear. As soon as the corn is ripe, he puts the sickle to it, because the harvest has come.*

We are told in the parable that the growth of the kingdom is likely to be slow. It is no one's fault that the seed grows slowly – this is simply the way it happens. So it follows that since healing is part of the outworking of God's kingdom, this too may also be a slow process. We may have a specific healing need which we feel is our top priority, but God may be more concerned about other parts of our lives. I believe that he is committed to bringing healing to every part of us, but not necessarily in the order in which we feel that it should take place.

16
CAN WE GET IN THE WAY?

We have just looked at the idea that God might have a different agenda for our healing, but could it also be that we might get in the way or be a stumbling block to our own prayers? The point about questioning this is not to have us raking through every aspect of our lives to see where the blockage might be, but rather to allow us to come before God in openness and ask him to transform us so that more of his glory might shine through us.

One issue might be our lack of confidence in coming before God. The reason for this could be due to any number of issues and is likely to be different for each person, but it is important to recognise what tends to sap our own confidence.

In Genesis 3:8, we read: 'Then the man and his wife heard the sound of the LORD God as he was walking in the garden in the cool of the day, and they hid from the LORD God among the trees of the garden.' The reason Adam and Eve hid was because they had just disobeyed God and were feeling afraid to face him, and it might be that at times we, as prayer ministers, feel similarly. When we are praying for others, it might be that something we have done wrong comes to mind and causes us to feel less confident that God is kindly disposed to our prayers.

Feeling out of our depth can also sap our confidence

Feeling out of our depth can also sap our confidence. It may be that we feel that the issue raised is far outside our realm of competence or perhaps simply that we are just too new to this ministry to be of much use. The vital thing to remember is that it is not actually us who does the healing, but Jesus working through us. Taking a little time to remind ourselves of this can be so helpful, and it is worth taking note of some verses from the Bible:

Do you not know that your bodies are temples of the Holy Spirit, who is in you, whom you have received from God? (1 Corinthians 6:19)

The thief comes only to steal and kill and destroy; I have come that they may have life, and have it to the full. (John 10:10)

The one who is in you is greater than the one who is in the world. (1 John 4:4)

You might find it helpful to write these down so that you can read them before you begin to pray for somebody and be reminded of the amazing truth contained within them.

It is probably the case that it is not so much that we get in the way of God and the person for whom we are praying, but more that we can get in the way of ourselves and God! The ministry of healing in the church would be in a very sorry state if we had to be perfect before we prayed for anyone, but if our confidence in God working through us is at a low ebb, we are unlikely to generate much faith for the person for whom we are praying. Building our confidence will have an effect upon our faith as we dare begin to believe that God can indeed work through us.

17
LISTENING TO WHAT GOD SAYS FOR OTHERS

I have been suggesting that one of the aims of praying for people in need is to let the person find something of Jesus' agenda as we pray for him or her. The question often asked is what are we, as prayer ministers, to do with whatever we feel the Spirit is saying to us when we are praying for someone else? Such promptings may well come in the form of 'pictures' that go through our minds, Bible verses that may come to us or indeed other ways in which we may sense God communicating with us. What do we do with such things? Let us first look at a number of reasons why these revelations might come to us instead of to the person for whom we are praying:

To say something that people could not hear for themselves

Every year I go to a meeting when a major part of that time is spent praying for each person individually. On one such occasion, somebody felt that they had a 'word' for me (along the lines of God's delight in me). I duly received this word, but dismissed it, thinking it didn't really have a big impact upon me – or perhaps I didn't let it have the impact I imagine God wanted it to have on me. However, when I returned to the same gathering exactly a year later and a different person had exactly the same word for me (delivered quite a bit more forcibly), I began to take more notice of it and explore what it might mean for God to delight in me.

We would all love to hear good things spoken about us by others and by God, but actually we more readily take to heart negative things. God has so many good things he wants to implant into us, but our problem is that we relegate most of them to the 'too good to be true' pile and don't take them seriously. When people give us good, encouraging 'words' they feel are from God, we should write them down and ask if God is trying to break through our negative self-image. It is interesting that if we kept a record of all the things God has spoken to us, we would probably find that he has been trying to say the same things for a long time.

To counter other voices that might be speaking

It may not literally be voices that are speaking to us, but certainly within us all there are thoughts and distractions turning us away from the voice of God. It may be an opinion about ourselves that has arisen because of what others may have said over the years or a belief that basically we are not really of much value compared to other people. All manner of events and conversations may have led to that suspicion taking root within us, and as we grow in our experience of hearing the voice of God, this doubt about who we are may still be there, dulling our sense of God's approval of us.

As we ponder the presence of 'other voices', we also have an enemy who is vocal in what he is whispering to us. The Bible describes the devil as one who, amongst other things, 'steals' (John 10:10). One of the things that he loves to steal from us is the knowledge of God's love for us. This usually takes the form of a voice that whispers something along the lines of, 'This isn't for you,' or 'God loves the whole world, but not you.'

Sometimes it can take a word brought to us by someone else to pierce these thoughts and bring us back to a more godly way of seeing ourselves.

Catching the intercession of Jesus and the Spirit

Romans 8 gives us two fascinating pictures of Jesus and the Spirit, both engaged in the same activity – praying, or interceding, for us.

The Spirit himself intercedes for us through wordless groans. (Romans 8:26)

Christ Jesus, who died – more than that, who was raised to life – is at the right hand of God and is also interceding for us. (Romans 8:34)

This is an aspect of intercession that we often overlook. It can be a very moving experience to learn that when we have been going through a particularly hard time there have been people praying for us. To know that we are prayed for and what those prayers are can be such an encouragement to us.

To know that we are prayed for and what those prayers are can be such an encouragement to us

When we are praying for people and something comes to us in those times, it is possible that what is happening is that we are catching something of the intercession of Jesus and the Holy Spirit for that person. When we pray for people, we are actually engaged in the same activity as that of Jesus and the Spirit – so would it not seem logical that they try to share their prayers with us so we would pray the same prayers as them? If this is what may be going on, it is probably wise to spend some time actually praying that picture into being by joining in with the prayers of heaven for that person.

To reveal something that might be hidden

It is obviously true to say that God knows everything and we do not! This truth is probably applicable to almost every area of life, and it is certainly one of the reasons why people may be hurting and suffering in the way they do. We often have no idea of the causes that might be behind the reactions we have and the things that we do. We have already noted that in the gospel accounts of Jesus healing the sick, it is remarkable how little he seemed to be interested in the causes of people's sicknesses and illnesses. Knowing the reasons why they were that way did not seem to be a part of their healing process. Similarly, it is probably true that we also do not need to know the reasons behind someone's suffering. However, there may be occasions when such knowledge or revelation is necessary and we can expect God, who knows all things, to reveal what is necessary for us to know.

> . . . we can expect God, who knows all things, to reveal what is necessary for us to know

Sharing what we receive

Just because we receive something, it may not necessarily be the case that we have to share it immediately. There are a number of reasons for this. First and foremost, we want the person to listen to God for himself or herself. The danger of revelation is that the prayer minister who receives something could be seen as having a special 'hot line' to God. Our desire is that people forge their own relationship with Jesus where they can encounter him for themselves and talk to and listen to him. This is the aim in any time of ministry, and the danger of rushing in to share whatever revelations we may have is that it can negate or diminish what the person may be hearing or beginning to hear from God.

Our practice is to let people encounter the presence of Jesus for themselves; to have that conversation with him that can be so liberating. After they have finished might be a good time to share what you have sensed Jesus may be saying, when what you share may complement what they were sensing or lead into a further time of prayer and encounter. In this way there is no suggestion that what we might have to say is in any way superior or more urgent than what they may have been sensing Jesus was saying to them. As with all revelations, it is good to write them down so that they are not forgotten as time passes.

18
WORKING TOGETHER AS A TEAM

Often we find ourselves as part of a team when we are praying for someone. It may be the practice of your church that people pray in pairs, and for many reasons this can be a good idea. If so, how can we best operate as a team together?

By and large, we are not very good at working together. Normally one person takes the lead and prays about everything that is on their heart, and when they have finished the second person chips in with all the things the first person has forgotten, or subtly seeks to correct any mistakes the first person made! Hardly a good use of team! Certainly when Paul speaks about the gifts of the Holy Spirit in 1 Corinthians 12, his emphasis is on people working together. The analogy he uses is that of a body and how each part of the body needs every other part.

When we come together to pray for someone in need, perhaps it is helpful to think in terms of planning to pray as a team, with each of the people prepared to bring something different to the time of prayer.

When we looked at the different elements that seemed to be present when Jesus ministered, we noted the three elements of encounter, faith and power. We also looked at how we can minister these elements more effectively. One way that we can operate as a team is to let different members of the team address these different elements. Perhaps one person could bring the person seeking prayer into an encounter with Jesus, and the other could address the elements of faith and power. Alternatively, one prayer minister could lead the encounter, one bring faith into the session, and then both could lay hands on the person and encourage the flow of God's power. It probably doesn't matter what each prayer minister does, as long as everyone works together as a team. All it takes is a quick decision at the beginning as to who is going to do what. The advantage of doing this is that each person on the ministry team has their own specific role, and each can play a part in leading and supporting.

19
INTERCESSION

Another way in which we are all involved in praying for people is when we intercede for them. It is quite possible to use this 'Father, Son, Spirit' approach to bring new life to our prayers of intercession.

Using 'Encounter' in Intercession

Father

As you begin to lift up someone in prayer, let the first step be to call to mind the Father's love for them, which is so deep and boundless that he sent Jesus to die for them.

Son

The next stage is to ask that question that can so often release a sense of the presence of Jesus – 'Where is Jesus for them right now?' Pay attention to what comes to mind. What is Jesus trying to say about his relationship with them? As you continue praying for them, share with Jesus whatever you feel you want to share. If you had a sense of where Jesus is in relation to that person, that in itself might prompt a specific prayer that you would like to pray. As with praying for people face-to-face, our communication with Jesus should not be a one-sided thing, but rather should prompt us to listen to what he is saying to us about them, which may in turn prompt further intercession from us.

Spirit

As you focus on the situation or person for whom you are praying, ask the Holy Spirit to be there and to bring what is needed. There is a lovely verse in Psalm 5:3 that reads: 'I lay my requests before you and wait expectantly.'

Hold on to an expectation that as you bring this situation or person to God, he will honour his promise and something will happen.

Bringing Faith to Our Intercession

When we were talking about faith previously, we approached it from the basis of asking four questions about the person for whom we are praying. It is a very easy step to apply those four questions to those for whom we intercede.

1. What does God think of this person?

Come back again to that wonderful sense of the Father's love for them. Remind yourself of the verse in 1 John 4:16, assuring you that you can know and rely on the love that God has for them.

2. What does God want for this person?

You might like to read again Jesus' mission statement in Luke 4:18–19:

The Spirit of the Lord is on me, because he has anointed me to proclaim good news to the poor. He has sent me to proclaim freedom for the prisoners and recovery of sight for the blind, to set the oppressed free, to proclaim the year of the Lord's favour.

Do any of the categories mentioned apply to the person in your prayers? Are they a prisoner because of something they have done? Is it sickness that is troubling them or are they weighed down by oppression of some sort? If so, the mission of Jesus is to bring good news, freedom, healing and release.

3. What has he already done for this person?

He has laid down his life in order that this person for whom you pray might have abundant life. He is that serious about them.

4. How can they find more?

As you pray for them, have confidence that it is God's will to pour out grace and mercy upon them in their time of need.

Drawing upon God's Power for Our Intercession

It is a slightly harder issue to convey power through intercession as we are not usually in a position to lay hands upon the recipient of our prayers. However, what we can do is to have the confidence to ask the Holy Spirit to pour himself out upon the person and that in doing so he will be the very touch of Jesus upon their life.

In his gospel, John writes a verse that is so important for us as we conclude our intercessory prayer. He writes: 'This is the confidence we have in approaching God: that if we ask anything according to his will, he hears us. And if we know that he hears us – whatever we ask – we know that we have what we asked of him' (1 John 5:14–15). It is an amazing thought that every prayer we have prayed has been heard by God and it is this that gives us great peace to believe in his healing touch upon those we lift to him.

20
FINAL THOUGHTS

The very thought of attempting to pray for someone and seek to bring them into the presence of Jesus may be utterly daunting and quite terrifying. We can be very quick to think of all the things we might do wrong. Perhaps the thing that inspires me most in this is the thought that Jesus' desire to meet with someone must far outweigh my desire for it. His love for them is greater than my imperfect love, and his desire for relationship is far greater than mine could ever be. With that in mind, I find that I can approach a time of prayer with the confidence that he wants this far more than I could ever want it, and all I have to do is to be there to help open the door between them.

. . . all I have to do is to be there to help open the door between them

The structure I have laid down is not a set of rules that has to be slavishly obeyed but, as I have already mentioned, is rather like setting a train on a set of tracks and allowing it to reach its destination in a good, relaxed manner. I am not suggesting that this was how Jesus prayed, but rather that it seems good to incorporate into our prayers what he seemed to incorporate in his: if he felt it was important to be among us, to increase faith and to call on the power of God, then perhaps we should follow his example.

Of course, there will be times when we will get everything wrong from a human perspective, but thankfully he does not rely on our perfection and can still work through our weakness. However, this is not a licence to be 'sloppy' and Paul's encouragement as far as spiritual gifts are concerned has much relevance here: he encourages us to 'try to excel' (1 Corinthians 14:12).

Perhaps one final thing to mention is that we do not minister as individual superstars who are out to change the world on our own! We are part of Christ's body, the church. We minister as part of the church, alongside others, and under the authority of others, with all the humility that requires. If you feel this is a ministry to which you are drawn, speak to someone in leadership and minister with their blessing alongside others. Part of the reason for this is that we need both the encouragement and the guidance of others that come through being a part of his wider body. Ultimately, of course, this is God's work and not ours, but it is a work in which he has called us to share with him. Joyfully, he is the senior partner!

APPENDICES

APPENDIX 1
SUMMARY OF MEDITATIONS

Speaking His Blessing Over Us

The LORD bless you and keep you;
the LORD make his face shine upon you
and be gracious to you;
the LORD turn his face towards you and give you peace.
(Numbers 6:24–26)

What we are seeking to do is to slowly take each phrase of this blessing and turn it back into a phrase of worship to God. The more we can put this into our own words, then the more personal it will be. Take the opening phrase – 'The LORD bless you'. You might want to begin with something along these lines:

Lord, I worship you whose heart's desire is to bless me.

I am sorry for those times when I see you as a punishing and unforgiving God.

I am sorry that I miss the love you have for me.

I worship you whose nature is to bless, to think well of me and to speak well of me.

Take each phrase and turn it into a time of worship to God.

Chosen, Adopted, Forgiven, Marked

It might be helpful to hold a cross as you ponder the four glorious truths of being chosen, adopted, forgiven and marked. We are going to hold onto each of the four 'arms' of the cross as we take time to specifically worship God for the truth of each of these words. The very act of holding onto, or touching, a different 'arm' for each of these words is that it can help us slow down and consciously dwell on each particular word.

Hold one of the 'arms' of the cross and worship God. Acknowledge that it is true you are personally chosen. The less we believe it to be true of ourselves, the more time we may need to spend on this particular truth.

The more personal we can make it, the better, but as a suggestion, it might be helpful to begin along these lines:

I worship you, Father, and thank you that you have chosen me.

You chose me before the foundation of the world.

Before I did one good thing, you chose me.

I worship you because you still choose me.

You promised never to reject me.

Carry on until something of this truth begins to touch you deeply. When you feel that it is appropriate, move your fingers to another 'arm' of the cross and begin to worship him for the truth that he has adopted you. Then move on to meditate on his forgiveness and for the truth that you are marked with his presence.

Practising Being a Name-bearer

I bear your name, Lord God Almighty. (Jeremiah 15:16)

Let's take this verse and use it as an exercise to deepen within us the awareness of the wonder of who dwells within us, and the implications of that for us and for those people with whom we come into contact.

- Find a quiet place and time and sit comfortably without any other distractions.

- As you slowly breathe in, let your breathing be accompanied by the words, 'I bear your name'.

- As you slowly breathe out, concentrate on the words, 'Lord God Almighty'.

- Keep the pattern going for up to five minutes, or even longer if you want.

There are a number of ways in which this can be helpful. In itself, it is a daily reminder of the truth that we so often forget, that we carry his presence with us wherever we go.

As you practise the exercise, it might be helpful to let the day ahead of you run through your mind, pondering the people you are going to meet, the places you will go to and the events you have planned. As you play through those situations with these words going through your mind, what you are doing is bringing each of those people and events into the awareness of the presence of God within you. It is not just that he will accompany you throughout the day, but that people will be actively meeting the presence of God through you.

If you practise this exercise at the end of the day, use the events of the day as the focus and a way of recognising his presence with you, even when you might not have been aware of it.

As this practice becomes more natural and familiar, the words will begin to run through your mind at other times of the day when you are not consciously praying, to bring you that reminder of who you really are and what you really carry within you.

This awareness can really make a difference to us. All of us need the grace of his presence in our lives. It may be that we have a difficult decision to make, or we may feel led to give something of ourselves beyond our natural abilities or resources. If we can begin by calling to mind the truth that we carry within us the name of the Lord God Almighty, our confidence and expectation will increase with the knowledge that it is not just us doing what we can, but him in us.

Practising Faith

You might find it helpful to hold a cross for this exercise.

As you hold the top 'arm', begin to worship Jesus as the revelation of the love of God. Worship the Father for his love for you, a love that compelled him to send Jesus for you. Worship Jesus for his willingness to come to this earth for you and to die for you. Let it become as personal as it can be.

Move to the second 'arm', and begin to worship Jesus for his mission of transformation. He came to bring fullness of life to you. Take a moment to consider those parts of your life where you would say that fullness is lacking, areas where you long to see his touch. Don't keep the focus on those things, but return to the wonder of his promise to transform.

Hold onto the third 'arm' and worship Jesus who laid down his life that you might have abundant life. Rejoice in prayer that Jesus has done everything to release abundant life into those areas of your life that need his touch.

Finally, as you hold the final 'arm' of the cross, be confident before him and ask him to bring his Holy Spirit to you to release his mercy and grace to you.

APPENDIX 2
ENCOUNTERING JESUS ON YOUR OWN

Before you begin a time of encounter, it might be worth taking a few deep breaths and consciously handing over to God anything that might be at the forefront of your mind so that you can let him do whatever he wants to do in this time.

The first stage is *Father*.

- Take a few minutes to let the words 'Abba, Father' go through your mind. Seek to catch the intimacy of a young child approaching the Father they love and trust. You might find it helpful to remind yourself that you were chosen before the foundation of the world, and that he chose to adopt you so he could pour out his love upon you.

- If past experience or the lack of a father's love is something that gets in the way, find in the person of Jesus a reflection of who the Father is. It might be necessary to break off and perhaps read one of the gospel stories about Jesus to let that story reveal something to you about the nature of God the Father.

- Try to stay with this stage until you sense a security in the love of God. This is not being self-indulgent; rather it is being obedient to the command of Jesus to remain in his love (John 15:9).

When you are comfortable in this place, move on to *Jesus, his Son*.

- Ask the Holy Spirit to bring you a glimpse of the person of Jesus and then ask yourself where Jesus is for you at that precise moment in time. The way you answer that question may well depend upon your personality, so there is certainly no right or wrong answer to this question.

- As you sit there, where would you say Jesus is? The sense that comes may even seem ridiculous or far-fetched, but stay with it and relax. It might seem a very distant or vague awareness but, again, stay with it however vague it may seem.

- Ask yourself how it feels to be in his presence. It is not just about letting Jesus be with us, it is also about giving ourselves permission to be there. Once again, savour the time spent in his presence. There is no need to rush to fill the moment with words – simply be there.

- When it feels right, speak to Jesus. What is it you want to say to him? Don't feel bound by what you feel you ought to say to him – say whatever is on your heart. Some people find it helpful to write down what they are saying. What this does is to create the expectation that he is going to speak to you.

- Let Jesus speak back to you. Hearing his voice is a matter of being aware of the spontaneous thoughts that come to you. What has come to your mind that was not there before? The 'voice' of Jesus may take the form of a seemingly random thought or a verse from the Bible.

- However it comes, write it down and give yourself time to ponder what he is saying. Develop this into a conversation, writing down your thoughts and questions to God, and recording what he is saying to you.

- It is good to pay attention to other things that might be happening, perhaps even physical touches of his presence.

- This is your encounter with Jesus. Take a moment to reflect on it.

What is the overall thing that you have come away with from this time?

How has it left you feeling?

What difference does it make to you?

The final stage is to focus on the person of the *Holy Spirit.*

- Approach him in the expectation that he desires to touch you and is willing to bring transformation.

- Have the confidence to believe that there is great power available for us who believe, the power of the Holy Spirit. Invite him to bring the touch of Jesus to you. It might help to put a hand where it hurts, or on your heart if your pain is emotional.

- Believe the truth that his power is at work in you.

APPENDIX 3
ENCOUNTERING JESUS WITH A GROUP

There are times when you may want to lead ministry for more than one person. This might take the form of a meditation at the beginning of a Bible study or small group meeting, or it could be part of a church service, possibly after the sermon or talk to allow people to engage with what has been said. I have come to call such times 'group encounters', occasions when people together can corporately be led into a time of finding God's presence for themselves.

Perhaps the best way of thinking about leading an 'encounter' is to think in terms of three spotlights that you are going to turn on, one at a time. The aim is to allow sufficient time for people to enjoy basking in the warmth from each particular spotlight in turn.

It may be best if the group begins by standing, but let everyone know that they are welcome to sit at any time. Standing seems to create an expectation that something is about to happen. Encourage the group to relax and put any concerns to one side for the moment.

1. The Light of the Love of 'Abba, Father'

Begin with a time of worship directed to the Father. Fix your own attention on him and begin to gently and audibly worship him for his fatherhood.

You might find it helpful to worship him for what he has done for all of us in one of the following ways:

- Psalm 139 – for his loving knowledge of who we are; he knows us completely, we are fearfully and wonderfully made and nothing we do can ever separate us from him.

- Ephesians 1 – there are four words that Paul used to describe how the Father sees us: *chosen* before the foundation of the world, *adopted* so that he can pour out his love upon us, *forgiven* by the work of Jesus on the cross and *marked* by the presence of the Holy Spirit.

- 2 Corinthians 1 – God is described as the Father of compassion and comfort; a description of him as the source of love, light and everything good.

- John 17:26 – God loves us with the same love that he has for Jesus, so the words of love he spoke over Jesus are the words of love he speaks over us:

    You are my beloved son / daughter

    I take pleasure in you.

2. The Light of the Presence of Jesus

Turn your attention to Jesus

In Galatians 2:20 Paul wrote about 'the Son of God, who loved me and gave himself for me'. Jesus promised in Matthew 28:20: 'I am with you always, to the very end of the age.' In his love for us Jesus promised to be with us, so we can be certain he is with each of us now.

Worship Jesus for his love for us

Take time to worship Jesus for his desire for intimacy with us all, and worship and honour him for everything that his death achieved, including the removal of everything that separated us from God. Worship him because he is present with each member of the group right now.

Give time for the Spirit to bring Jesus in any way that he chooses

Try to avoid the temptation to 'force' people into the encounter with Jesus that you want them to have.

Ask the group where Jesus is for them

Ask the question: *"Where is Jesus for you right now?"*

It might be helpful to give a range of possibilities – not to force their feelings in any way, but to give 'permission' to what they may be experiencing. Such suggestions might include:

● Is Jesus beside them, around them or within them?

● Is he in a different place altogether?

Let each person explore their answer

You are not asking people to imagine Jesus or to visualise him – you are letting Jesus reveal his presence in whatever way he chooses to do so.

Give time for this so that everyone can find Jesus wherever he might be.

Give the group the time and opportunity to engage with Jesus

The idea is that people are encouraged to move from simply experiencing his presence, to allowing Jesus to connect with them and them to connect with him.

Asking gentle questions and giving time for people to inwardly respond to them can assist this connection.

- Wherever Jesus might be – what is he like, or how does his presence feel?

- What does it feel like to be so close to him?

- What is he showing people about himself?

What is it that they would like to say to Jesus?

Invite each person to say whatever they wish to Jesus.

An encounter with Jesus is not just an experience of his presence, but also a chance to speak to him and receive from him. When the group is engaging with the presence of Jesus as much as possible, encourage them to tell him whatever is on their hearts. Jesus invited Bartimaeus to be bold in his requests (Mark 10:51), so encourage them – as Jesus stands there – what do they want to say to him?

What is Jesus revealing to them?

The next stage of this encounter is to allow each person to receive from Jesus. This might happen in a number of ways:

- Jesus might speak to them. Many people don't think that they can hear Jesus! However, his voice is often not a voice at all but can be like a spontaneous thought that comes to mind. Encourage each person to explore this as it may be the voice of Jesus for them. They may want to carry on in conversation with him.

- Jesus may speak through a picture, so encourage them to explore this.

- He may bring to mind a verse from the Bible or a song.

- Jesus might do something, such as bringing healing or a comforting touch.

3. The Light of the Power of the Holy Spirit

Invite the Holy Spirit to come. He is, of course, already present but you are asking him to come in a fresh way as he brings new things to the group. What you are seeking here is the power of the Holy Spirit to bring a living touch of Jesus.

When you have asked the Spirit to come, wait quietly in the expectation that he will certainly come, as Jesus promised he would in Luke 11:13. The work of the Holy Spirit can be quiet and gentle, almost unseen by the onlooker, or it can be dramatic and sometimes strange. However he chooses to work may not be an indication of the depth of what he is doing.

Encourage each person to be aware of the Holy Spirit's desire to bring transformation. Encourage them to try to be aware of anything that might be happening within them.

At all times remain worshipful, keeping your own eyes upon Jesus and allowing plenty of time for silence.

When the time feels right, draw the session to a close

When you, as leader, feel that the process is drawing to an end, gently ask people to begin to 'come to' and re-engage with the group. Encourage them to write down what they have just experienced as there is a real tendency to forget the wonders that God shares with us.

It can be helpful and very encouraging if individuals are willing to share their experience of encountering Jesus.

With a little practice you will soon become adept at fitting the group encounter into whatever time you have available, whether it be a few minutes or a longer period of time.

On occasions you may want to invite people to meet together specifically for the purpose of encountering God, and it's possible to spend around an hour doing this. If so, I hope the following suggestions may prove helpful:

- Someone needs to lead the group and be responsible for moving it along. Make sure that there is a comfortable room set aside, without distractions.

- Set aside 50–60 minutes for the session (although you can lead a shorter session if you wish).

- Don't worry about candles or music – the aim is to facilitate an encounter with God, and other visual/audio input can distract from this. There is a place for these in meditation, but that is different from what we are trying to do here.

- The number in the group does not matter. Anything from three to 300 people or more is fine!

- Make sure everyone has paper and a pen so they can write down what happens.

A suggested timetable for a longer group encounter might be as follows:

Welcome, introductions and explanation	5 minutes
Setting the scene	15 minutes

Include:

- switching off from the day

- handing any concern or anxiety over to God so that people can relax and receive his peace

- reading a gospel story – perhaps a healing story – and perhaps asking each person to share one thing that strikes them from it.

Leading the encounter meditation	15 minutes
Opportunity for people to make their own notes	10 minutes
Time for sharing (if the size and make-up of the group allows)	10 minutes
Final act of worship / blessing	5 minutes

Such times of group encounter can be extremely powerful, and I have known many people testify to physical healing without anyone praying for them or laying hands on them in any way.

Sometimes it might seem right to move from a time of encounter to ministry, and a gentle way of doing this is to have two or three people present who have the confidence and gentleness to move round the group and silently lay hands upon each person in turn. It really is not necessary for any words to be spoken. In fact, in such times our words can break into and spoil what is going on between God and the person receiving.

People who are ministering might find it helpful to silently pray the Lord's Prayer over each person. They may also find it helpful to catch the truth of what is happening; namely, that the Holy Spirit within them is flowing into those upon whom they are laying hands. Such gentle healing ministry can prove to be very powerful and effective.

APPENDIX 4
GUIDELINES FOR MINISTRY

These guidelines for ministry are enclosed as a suggestion for a church or a group to follow. They have been formulated after many years of experience, and allow for healing prayer ministry to take place in a number of settings.

Fundamental issues

- There is a difference between prayer ministry and counselling. In prayer ministry, our central focus is to bring the person coming for ministry (referred to throughout as 'the visitor') into an awareness of the presence of God, and to seek the healing that flows from that.

- This healing ministry involves offering loving acceptance, non-judgemental listening, sensitive responses, discernment and patience, as well as an openness to the leading of the Holy Spirit, and while we are all on our own journeys of being transformed into the likeness of Jesus, those who undertake this ministry should demonstrate these abilities prior to being allowed to minister. Ministry should be under the authority of church leadership. If there is the possibility of praying with children, prayer ministers should be subject to the usual checks that are commonplace in other areas of the church's ministry.

Differences in style

Ministry can take place in a wide variety of formats and places: as a drop-in, after church services, in a setting where appointments are made, or a combination of these. It may take place in one large room, with ministry happening in various parts of the room, or in a setting where smaller, more private places of ministry are available. It is hoped that these guidelines can be applied to all the various options available.

General principles

- If ministering in a private setting, there should always be two prayer ministers with each visitor, at least one of them of the same sex as the visitor.

- It is impossible to promise total confidentiality to those seeking ministry, as this will need to be broken if required by law, or if there is a risk of danger to themselves or others.

- We do believe in the practice of the laying on of hands, but permission should always be sought first, and touch should generally be limited to the head and shoulders. If it feels right to lay hands on a specific part of the visitor's body (as in the case of physical healing), then such laying on of hands should only be done by a member of the same sex as the visitor after they have sought permission from the visitor, and regard must always be paid to what is seen to be appropriate.

- It is beneficial for prayer ministers to keep their eyes open while praying to watch what may be happening.

- It is important that we do not overstep our authority as far as the medical world is concerned (for whom we have a high regard). People should be encouraged not to make any changes to their medication without seeing their doctors.

- We believe that it is God's will to heal, and prayers for healing should be offered accordingly and not apologetically. However, while we are seeking to pray in faith, we must avoid making any promises as to exactly how or when healing will come. Much disappointment and anger can arise when we promise things on God's behalf.

The content of a prayer ministry session

- Sometimes ministry can take place effectively without the visitor sharing their story, but when the visitor is invited to share, it is useful for clarifying the healing issue.

- Whatever format ministry takes, it is always useful to spend time seeking to engage with the presence of God. We have found it helpful to begin any time of prayer by focusing on the presence of God rather than focusing immediately on the issues raised by the visitor.

- Our experience is that prayer ministry need not be a wordy matter, but much is accomplished by allowing the Holy Spirit to work in times of quiet.

- If the prayer ministers sense that they are being given words or pictures, discernment is required whether to share these with the visitor. If appropriate, attention should be given to:

  - the timing: it may be better to give words and pictures at the end, as the person may be experiencing God in a different way and our words might be a distraction. Once we share, it is always possible to lead into more ministry time if appropriate.

  - how such words or pictures might be received if we fail to speak them with sufficient gentleness.

  - the benefit of writing them down so the person can remember them more clearly afterwards.

- Healing is often a process of transformation, and it is good to encourage visitors to return for more prayer if it seems appropriate. Part of the transformation process may be that God brings healing to another part of the visitor's life other than the original healing issue raised.

Good practice in ministry

It is good if some form of supervision can be offered on a regular basis to all prayer ministers (where they can raise any difficulties they may have faced), and to ensure that they have a team leader to speak to if necessary so that no-one goes home feeling burdened by their experience of ministry.

All of us find ourselves going through hard times, and the prayer ministers themselves may need support from time to time. We know that God can use imperfect people, but it is important for those ministering to be responsible for their own lives and to seek help when it is needed.

Prayer ministers are not there to offer advice.

Praying for children

- Before a child receives prayer in the context of private prayer ministry, permission must be sought from their parents and we would expect a parent or a designated adult to be present during sessions.

- Keep your language simple and short when you are praying, and generally keep the prayer times short. This will help with a child's understanding.

- If a child/young person becomes distressed, stop praying and reassess the situation.

The Christian Healing Mission works with churches and individuals of all denominations. It is committed to visiting churches and building relationships as it encourages them in this ministry. CHM also welcomes those in need of prayer at its premises in London, and has various means of enabling people to receive ministry nationwide – please contact the Mission for details.

At the heart of all the material produced by CHM is the message of 'Encounter Prayer'. The full range of resources can be found on the Mission's website **www.healingmission.org**.
This includes details of John Ryeland's other books, as well as material for you to read, listen to, watch, download or participate in – much of which is free.

THE CHRISTIAN HEALING MISSION

8 Cambridge Court
210 Shepherds Bush Road
London W6 7NJ
020 7603 8118
chm@healingmission.org
www.healingmission.org

Charity Registration: 1080534 | Company Registration: 3877993